THE MONTESSORI METHOD
Simplified

Written
by

Kim Suzuki

© Copyright 2024 - All rights reserved.

The content contained within this book may not be reproduced, duplicated or transmitted without direct written permission from the author or the publisher.

Under no circumstances will any blame or legal responsibility be held against the publisher, or author, for any damages, reparation, or monetary loss due to the information contained within this book, either directly or indirectly.

Legal Notice:

This book is copyright protected. It is only for personal use. You cannot amend, distribute, sell, use, quote or paraphrase any part, or the content within this book, without the consent of the author or publisher.

Disclaimer Notice:

Please note the information contained within this document is for educational and entertainment purposes only. All effort has been executed to present accurate, up to date, reliable, complete information. No warranties of any kind are declared or implied. Readers acknowledge that the author is not engaged in the rendering of legal, financial, medical or professional advice. The content within this book has been derived from various sources. Please consult a licensed professional before attempting any techniques outlined in this book.

By reading this document, the reader agrees that under no circumstances is the author responsible for any losses, direct or indirect, that are incurred as a result of the use of the information contained within this document, including, but not limited to, errors, omissions, or inaccuracies.

TABLE OF CONTENTS

INTRODUCTION 7

01. RESPECT FOR THE CHILD 11
Respect for the Child: A Foundation for Independence. 11
Observation with Minimal Intervention........... 13
Freedom Within Limits: Crafting a Safe Exploration Space. 16
Respectful Discipline: Balancing Kindness and Boundaries........................ 19
Building Relationships: Connection Over Control .23

02. THE ABSORBENT MIND. 27
Sensitive Periods. 28
Hands-On Learning: Connecting the Neural Dots. .31
Nature as a Classroom: Incorporating the Outdoors 33
Choosing Developmentally Appropriate Toys. 35
DIY Montessori Materials: Budget-Friendly Solutions.. 37

03. SELF-DIRECTED LEARNING. 41
Creating Individualized Learning Paths: Tailored Approaches 44
Milestones and Natural Pace: Avoiding Comparison Traps.. 48

Encouraging Intrinsic Motivation: Cultivating
Curiosity..50
Observation Techniques......................52

04. HOLISTIC DEVELOPMENT................55
Cognitive Development..........................56
Physical Development: Building Strength and
Coordination..59
Language and Communication Skills............61
Practical Life Skills: Everyday Learning
Opportunities.......................................63
Emotional Development: Building Emotional
Intelligence and Resilience 65
Social Skills: Cultivating Respectful Interactions....67
Problem-Solving Abilities: Encouraging Critical
Thinking..70
Math and Numeracy : Unlocking the Secret Code..73
Botany and Zoology : Cultivating Relationships With
the Living 74
Geography and Cosmology: Broadening the
Definition of "Home" 75

05. SETTING UP YOUR HOME 79
The Bedroom..80
The Kitchen 83
The Play Area 85
The Bathroom.......................................89
The Entryway 92
Visuals and Diagrams 95

06. DAILY ROUTINES THE MONTESSORI WAY 99
Examples of Montessori-Infused Daily Routines..102
Tips to Increase the Success of Daily Routines....107
Balancing Montessori with Other Parenting Styles 111

Crafting a Personalized Montessori Plan 112

CONCLUSION. 115

ACTIVITIES LIST. 121
    Notes on the Activities List 122
    0-12 MONTHS 123
    12-24 MONTHS. 142
    2 TO 3 YEARS 157
    3 TO 4 YEARS 173
    4 TO 5 YEARS 189

MARIA MONTESSORI'S ORIGINAL LEARNING MATERIALS.. 215

REFERENCES.. 221

INTRODUCTION

"It is not true, that I invented what is called The Montessori Method. I have studied the child, I have taken what the child has given me and expressed it, and that is what is called The Montessori Method."

-Maria Montessori

As a busy parent, juggling work and home life, I know exactly what millions of parents like me desire in a parenting guide; a proven method that makes sense to them, plus simple and clear actionable steps to make it work.

Today, parents like you and me face a mountain of challenges. We want the best for our children, but we're pulled in so many directions. Work demands a big chunk of our time and energy, the house needs our care, and we still want to create a nurturing environment for our little ones, and spend quality time with them while time flies by at an unbelievable pace. The pressure is immense, and it only grows with the endless stream of conflicting advice on parenting. Add the consumerist push to buy more and do more, and it's no wonder we feel overwhelmed.

This is where the Montessori Method shines as a bright beacon of clarity and purpose, providing not only an optimal path for our children's fulfillment, but also some of what parents need the most; the opportunity to breathe, and simply enjoy the moments they share with their children. Through Montessori, we realize that being a *good parent* or *good teacher* does not necessarily mean doing more for our children, it actually means doing less, but in a very specific way. We learn that by creating a specific type of environment for the child, all the qualities that we consider to be good in humans seem to naturally flourish in and out of them. Indeed, this represents a bold promise—one that Dr. Montessori and her method have first demonstrated to the world more than a century ago.

Although the original written work of Maria Montessori makes a very interesting read for the intellectual and scientific types among us, it is clearly not for everybody. This book is here to simplify the Montessori method, making it accessible to any parent from any background. Its purpose is to provide clear, actionable guidance that fits into a busy life. I want these principles to be accessible and inspiring, helping parents to integrate them into daily routines with ease.

The structure of the book is straightforward. It begins with an understanding of the four core principles—respect for the child, the absorbent mind, self-directed learning, and holistic development. You'll then find practical guidance on setting up a Montessori home and daily routines with your children, followed by an extensive activities list, organized by age group and activity type. Each chapter builds on the last, guiding you from understanding to implementation. Although the list of activities is quite substantial, I still give many examples of activities throughout the book, to better clarify some of the ideas that are being conveyed. Also, to both further your understanding of the method and to inspire you in providing your child with purposeful toys and materials, I have included a list of the original didactic materials used by Maria Montessori at the end of the book. You are welcome to jump to those lists whenever you feel your own curiosity and creativity speak to you.

By drawing on Maria Montessori's teachings, this book offers guidance that is both reputable and sensible. Here, you'll find a path that stands apart from the noise—clear, trustworthy, and easy to follow. Although this guide aims to be as concise as possible, I promise that you have everything here to bring the timeless Montessori principles into your life. The rest will depend on your willingness to act on this information and implement the ideas into your own family dynamic and home space.

It is my sincere wish that you feel empowered by this book. With it, you can create a harmonious home environment that supports your child's holistic development, and also feel completely fulfilled as a parent. So, dear parent, let's take this step together confidently, and let the magic of Montessori begin!

CHAPTER 1
RESPECT FOR THE CHILD

"As a rule, however, we do not respect our children. We try to force them to follow us without regard to their special needs. We are overbearing with them, and above all, rude; and then we expect them to be submissive and well-behaved, knowing all the time how strong is their instinct of imitation and how touching their faith in and admiration of us. They will imitate us in any case. Let us treat them, therefore, with all the kindness which we would wish to help to develop in them."

-Maria Montessori

Respect for the Child: A Foundation for Independence

Promoting real-life skills is where it all begins. At this stage, Respect lies at the heart of the Montessori philosophy, and it begins with viewing your child as a complete person. This means recognizing that even the youngest children have their own thoughts, feelings, and opinions. It's about acknowledging their emotions and taking them seriously, fostering an environment where their voices matter. In practice, this respect translates to adapting our language to show empathy and understanding. It means speaking with them, not at them, and valuing their input in family decisions. When a child feels respected, they learn to respect themselves and others.

One of the most impactful ways to promote independence is through respecting your child's autonomy. This involves making your home a space where they can explore and learn safely. Lower shelves and furniture they can use independently empower them to make choices about their activities. Encouraging self-care routines, like dressing and feeding, not only builds practical skills but also confidence. When children are given the tools and opportunities to do things on their own, they develop a sense of ownership, responsibility, and independence.

Understanding that each child develops at their own pace is another key aspect of respect. Every child is unique, with their own interests and abilities. Observing without judgment allows us to provide opportunities for self-directed play, where children can explore their passions at their own speed. It's about offering a range of activities and letting them decide what captures their interest. This approach respects their individuality and also supports their natural growth and learning processes. By giving them the freedom to focus on what they love, we nurture their creativity, problem-solving skills, and an everlasting love for learning.

Maria Montessori recognized very clearly the immense intelligence that is already present in the child at birth and only waiting to expand and express itself in various ways as the child gains information from the outside world. It becomes our role, then, to respect this seed of infinite potential and provide an environment where it can bloom and operate its own magic. This reality may be hard for us parents to integrate at first, since we may be attached to the idea that we are the ones making the good stuff happen for our children. But as we learn to embrace our true place and role in the child's development, we learn that there is no greater honor than being the invisible hero, the silent guardian of that which is most precious.

It's imperative to see our children as capable individuals, deserving of the same respect we afford adults. By embracing this mindset, we create an environment where children can thrive, explore their world, and develop into independent, confident individuals. This foundation of respect sets the stage for all the other principles we'll explore in this book, offering a path to a more harmonious and fulfilling parenting experience.

Observation with Minimal Intervention

> *"It is necessary for the teacher to guide the child without letting him feel his or her presence too much, so that she may be always ready to supply the desired help, but may never be the obstacle between the child and his experience."*
>
> -Maria Montessori,
> *Dr. Montessori's Own Handbook*

How does one effectively observe a child? It starts by creating a space that invites exploration without the need for constant oversight. This means setting up an environment where your child feels safe to roam and investigate. Think about how you can arrange your home to encourage this freedom. Maybe it's a corner of the living room with soft mats and lower shelves with a few purposeful toys, or a child-sized table where they can engage in art or puzzles. With this setup, you can step back, allowing your child the room to make decisions and learn from their environment. It might feel counterintuitive at first, especially if you're used to guiding every step. However, stepping back and respecting your child's autonomy is key to fostering independence.

Recognizing developmental milestones happens more clearly through observation. When you watch your child without the pressure to intervene, you begin to notice patterns and milestones. You see when they first attempt to stack blocks or when they show interest in turning book pages. You notice when they become just a little more efficient at something, or when they unlock the next level of a complex activity they have been practicing for the past few weeks. These moments provide insight into their developmental progress, areas of interest, and the sensitive periods the child might find themselves in (more on this later). They inform you of when to introduce new challenges or when to step back even further and let them struggle and succeed on their own. This patient observation is a powerful tool, allowing you to support your child's learning journey without imposing your own timeline or agenda.

There's another layer to observation: the relationship it builds between you and your child. As you spend time observing, you become more attuned to their needs and interests. This attunement strengthens your bond, creating a relationship based on understanding and trust. Your child feels seen and valued. This foundation of trust is priceless, fostering a sense of security and confidence in your child. They learn that they can explore their world, knowing you are there to support them without overwhelming their space.

Yet, even with the best intentions, the urge to intervene can be strong. It's natural to want to help, to guide, and to protect. However, constantly stepping in can stifle a child's growth. In Maria Montessori's words : "Praise, help, or even a look, may be enough to interrupt him, or destroy the activity..." To overcome this impulse of chiming in, mindfulness practices can be incredibly helpful. Take a moment to breathe, to ground yourself, and to commit to observation only. Remember that your role is not to lead every activity but to provide a safe space for exploration. By practicing mindfulness, you learn to trust in your child's capabilities, allowing them to learn from their experiences, successes, and even their mistakes. There are numerous benefits to being a passive and alert observer when you are with your child. If you have not experienced those benefits yet, I wholeheartedly encourage you to give it a sincere try, and discover those hidden-in-plain-sight treasures for yourself;)

In the end, observation is about letting go of the need to control every moment. It's about trusting the process, trusting your child, and trusting yourself. It requires patience and practice, but the rewards are profound. You not only support your child's journey toward independence but also enrich your own understanding and connection with them. As you embrace observation, you'll find that it transforms not just your approach to parenting, but your relationship with your child, laying the groundwork for a mutual respect and trust.

Freedom Within Limits: Crafting a Safe Exploration Space

> *"To let the child do as he likes when he has not yet developed any powers of control, is to betray the idea of freedom ... . Real freedom, instead, is a consequence of development; it is the development of latent guides, aided by education."*
>
> - Maria Montessori,
> *The Absorbent Mind*

Picture a child in a safe and inviting playground, the world at their feet, eager to climb, jump, and explore. This image beautifully captures the Montessori concept of *freedom within limits*. It's about finding that delicate balance where children can roam freely yet safely, discovering their capabilities within a structured environment. Boundaries in this context aren't about restriction, but rather serve as guides that help children understand their world. They provide security and a framework within which children can make choices. When we explain the purpose of boundaries to our children, we demystify these limits, turning them into allies rather than adversaries. By setting clear boundaries and offering choices within them, we foster decision-making skills and self-discipline. For instance, allowing a child to choose between two healthy snacks encourages autonomy while maintaining nutritional boundaries. This approach respects their independence and ensures that their explorations are safe and manageable.

Designing a safe exploratory environment is where creativity meets practicality. Think about the spaces in your home that your child frequents. Are they conducive to exploration? Child-proofing is the first step, ensuring safety in every nook and cranny. This might mean securing furniture, covering electrical outlets, or using gates to limit access to potentially dangerous areas. But beyond safety, these spaces should encourage curiosity and learning. Clearly defined activity areas—like a reading corner, an art station, or a puzzle zone—help children navigate their environment with intention. Each area acts as a catalyst for different types of exploration and learning, allowing the child to choose where their interests lie at any given moment. These zones can be as simple or elaborate as space and resources allow but should always be inviting and accessible to the child. The key is to create an environment where they can engage freely, moving from one activity to another with ease.

Encouraging exploration and risk-taking is vital for a child's growth. While the word "risk" might raise eyebrows, in the Montessori context, it refers to calculated risks—challenges that push the child's boundaries just enough to foster growth without compromising safety. Outdoor play is an excellent avenue for such exploration, offering a natural environment where children can test their physical abilities. Climbing a tree, balancing on a low wall, or playing in the mud are activities that teach coordination, build strength, and instill confidence. These experiences are invaluable, teaching lessons that are not easily replicated indoors. Similarly, activities that challenge physical abilities, like obstacle courses or simple sports, encourage children to understand and push their limits. These activities build resilience and adaptability, qualities that are essential for navigating life's challenges.

Monitoring without hovering is an art that requires patience and trust. Again, it's about observing your child's explorations from a distance, providing the space they need to grow and learn independently. This doesn't mean disengaging but rather being present without being intrusive. The goal is to foster an environment where the child feels free to make mistakes and learn from them. Intervening only when necessary allows the child to develop problem-solving skills and resilience. It's a delicate balance but one that pays off significantly in independence development. Parents need to trust in their child's abilities and instincts, stepping in only when safety is at risk or when guidance is genuinely needed. This approach builds confidence in the child, knowing that they have the freedom to explore, with a safety net in place should they need it.

In this way, freedom within limits becomes a powerful tool in our parenting method, supporting a child's natural desire to explore while ensuring they remain safe and secure. It respects their individuality and capacity for growth, providing a structured yet flexible framework for learning. By crafting a safe environment and allowing for exploration, we empower our children to become confident, capable, and independent learners, ready to take on the world with curiosity and courage.

Respectful Discipline: Balancing Kindness and Boundaries

> *"I saw children with their feet on the tables, or with their fingers in their noses, and no intervention was made to correct them. I saw others push their companions, and I saw dawn in the faces of these an expression of violence; and not the slightest attention on the part of the teacher. Then, I had to intervene to show with what absolute rigour it is necessary to hinder, and little by little suppress, all those things which we must not do, so that the child may come to discern clearly between good and evil."*
>
> - Maria Montessori,
> *The Montessori Method*

The word *rigour* used by Maria Montessori in the quote above is not used to mean *harshness* or *severity*, but rather *thoroughness* and *consistency*. In response to the strict discipline experienced under authoritarian parenting, many parents today lean towards the other extreme; fostering an environment of unguided freedom that leads to confusion and unclear boundaries. The vital discernment between *good and evil*, as Dr. Montessori puts it, is a lesson that children do not learn, in the cases of libertarian parenting, until they are older and meet the vivid backlash of society for a behavior that was not addressed at home during the first formative years. I have seen many parents who have made the unwavering commitment to never alter their tone of voice while speaking to their child. Although the initial intention of the parent is to never shout at the child, the vast amount of information that is conveyed through the variation of pitch, tone and volume in the voice is also lost in the process. The successful transmission of the information from the parent to their child then becomes solely dependent on the meaning of the words alone, while we know that the vocabulary of the child who is under 4 years of age is still very limited. It is imperative then that the child benefit from this kind of emotional feedback from the parent. First, for the child to become proficient at discerning what is accepted and what is not. Second, so they can benefit from a mature modeling of how to manage emotions.

Does being respectful at all times mean we have to act like emotionless robots? Of course not. If you want your child to learn how to express their emotions in a healthy way, you have to show them how it's done. "Mommy is angry because she doesn't like having juice spilled all over her on purpose." It's okay to let the energy of your emotion flow through your voice to a certain degree, so that you give the child a chance to understand what you are feeling. Most importantly, they will also record the fact that you remained calm and respectful while expressing yourself. This is the kind of model we want to give the child. That being said, if you feel like the emotion is too strong for you to express it with composure at the moment, it's better to remove yourself from the situation until you settle down, and have the conversation later. Again, letting your child know how they make you feel when they do certain things helps them understand boundaries. Do not deprive them of those precious lessons by thinking that parenting is about being a super human who has transcended emotions altogether. Show them that it's okay to feel emotions, and that there is a way to express it with respect and maturity.

Disciplining a child with empathy is about connecting with your child on a deeper level, guiding their behavior through understanding and compassion. It starts with listening—really listening—to what your child is trying to communicate. Children have a lot to say, even if they don't always have the words. By actively listening to their concerns, you show them that their feelings matter, that they are heard and valued. Reflecting their feelings back to them, you help them name and process their emotions, which is a crucial step in emotional development. If a child tries to push another child off the kicking horse, and then starts to cry when you intervene, you can offer warm support for a moment, and then say "I see you're sad because you want to play on the rocking horse too. Let's see if we can find a solution together." Don't go into the lengthy teaching lesson right away. When the child is in the midst of emotion, his capacity to listen attentively is extremely limited. Try to handle the conflict with as little words as possible. When the dust has settled, sit down with the child and reflect on what happened. Empathy doesn't mean letting children do whatever they want. It means putting yourself in their shoes, helping them understand the impact of their actions, and teaching them how to handle situations appropriately.

Setting boundaries is an essential part of empathetic discipline. Try to see boundaries not as a hindrance or necessary sacrifice, but rather a valuable gift to the child when used appropriately. Boundaries offer children security and predictability, helping them understand the world around them. It's important to use clear, concise language when setting these boundaries. Instead of saying, "Don't do that," specify what behavior is expected: "We use gentle hands with our friends." Consistency is key. Children feel secure when they know what to expect, which is why consistent consequences for actions are vital. This doesn't mean harsh punishment. Instead, it involves intervening everytime a line is crossed, and not just once in a while when you really had enough. It also involves using natural consequences that help children learn about cause and effect. For example, if a child spills their drink, they can help clean it up. This teaches responsibility without shaming and connects actions with outcomes in a practical way.

Modeling respectful behavior is another important aspect of empathetic discipline. Children learn so much from watching the adults in their lives. By demonstrating respect and patience in your interactions, you set a powerful example for your child. This means showing them how to treat others with kindness, even in challenging situations. It also means admitting when you're wrong and apologizing. When children see adults owning up to their mistakes, they learn that it's okay to be imperfect, that growth is a lifelong process. By being a role model, you teach them valuable life skills that go beyond any single lesson.

Courtesy into daily life helps children develop social skills and respectful behaviors. These lessons are not about rigid manners but about understanding how to interact with others kindly and considerately. Role-playing social scenarios can be a fun and effective way to teach these skills. For instance, you can act out a playdate scenario, guiding your child through how to share toys or express their feelings if they're upset. Teaching polite expressions and behaviors, like saying "please" and "thank you," helps children navigate social interactions smoothly. These small practices build a foundation for empathy and respect, essential traits for thriving in any community.

As you navigate the complexities of respectful discipline, remember that it's a balance of kindness and boundaries. It's about guiding children with love, helping them understand themselves and the world around them. This approach doesn't eliminate challenges, but it transforms them into opportunities for growth and connection. When children feel understood and respected, they learn to extend the same empathy to others. In this way, discipline becomes a form of teaching, nurturing not just compliance but genuine understanding and compassion.

Building Relationships: Connection Over Control

Think about the last time you shared a genuine laugh with your child. Those moments are more than just fleeting joy—they're the foundation of a strong, trusting relationship. When we prioritize connection over control, we create bonds that foster security and mutual respect. This starts with carving out daily one-on-one time with your child. In our busy lives, it's easy to overlook these moments, but they are crucial. Whether it's a few minutes before bed or a morning chat over breakfast, these interactions show your child that they are valued and loved. It doesn't have to be anything elaborate—just time spent together, without distractions, can work wonders. Engaging in child-led activities is another powerful way to build connection. Let your child take the lead in choosing what to play or explore. This boosts their confidence and deepens your understanding of their world. As they guide the activity, you see what excites them, what challenges them, and what brings them joy.

Open communication is the backbone of any healthy relationship, and it's no different with children. Effective communication goes beyond just talking; it involves truly listening. Make it a point to practice active listening. This means giving your full attention when your child speaks, maintaining eye contact, and showing genuine interest in what they're saying. It's about being present, in the moment, even if the topic seems trivial to adult ears. Encourage your child to express their thoughts and feelings openly. Create an environment where they feel safe to share without fear of judgment or dismissal. Ask open-ended questions that invite more than yes or no answers, prompting them to delve into their emotions and ideas. This practice builds their communication skills and reinforces their sense of self-worth.

One of the most effective ways to guide behavior is through connection. When children feel connected to their caregivers, they are more likely to respond positively to guidance. Use this connection to redirect behavior when needed. Instead of issuing commands, engage in shared activities that naturally guide them towards better choices. For instance, if your child is restless, instead of telling them to calm down, suggest a game or activity that channels their energy constructively. Humor and play can also be valuable tools in addressing challenges. A silly face or funny voice can defuse tension and redirect focus away from conflict, creating a more positive atmosphere. Through connection, discipline becomes less about control and more about collaboration, where both parties work together to find solutions.

Shared experiences strengthen bonds in ways words often cannot. They create memories and build a sense of belonging. Consider family cooking projects as a means to connect. Involve your child in meal preparation, from selecting recipes to measuring ingredients. This transforms a routine chore into a collaborative and educational experience. As you cook, conversations flow naturally, and skills are developed without the pressure of formal learning. Collaborative storytelling is another engaging activity that fosters connection. Start a story and let your child add the next part, taking turns until you've woven a tale together. This not only stimulates creativity but also encourages active listening and cooperation. These shared experiences provide a foundation of trust and security, reinforcing the idea that you are a team, navigating life's challenges together.

In the world of parenting, it's easy to fall into the trap of seeking control, but true influence comes from connection. By prioritizing strong relationships with our children, we lay the groundwork for mutual respect and understanding. These connections become the guiding force in our interactions, allowing us to navigate challenges with empathy and collaboration. As we focus on building these bonds, we create an environment where our children feel valued, heard, and loved—a place where they can thrive emotionally and socially.

CHAPTER 2
THE ABSORBENT MIND

Do you remember the first time your child skillfully pronounced a word, and you had no idea where they heard it? Or when they confidently completed a task that you never showed them how to do? These seemingly simple moments, brimming with curiosity and wonder, are not just milestones, but also reflections of what Maria Montessori describes as the *absorbent mind*. In these early years, children possess an extraordinary capacity to absorb knowledge from their surroundings, almost effortlessly. This chapter delves into the concept of sensitive periods—those magical windows of heightened receptivity where children are particularly attuned to specific types of learning. Recognizing and responding to these periods can greatly enhance their development, making your role as a parent both rewarding and impactful.

Sensitive Periods

Sensitive periods are times when your child is especially eager to learn certain skills, such as language or order. Imagine your child as a sponge, soaking up every sound and nuance of language in their environment. This is the language acquisition phase, a sensitive period where they are primed to pick up words, sounds, and eventually, whole sentences. Similarly, young children often crave order and routine, a sensitive period marked by an intense desire for predictability. This need for structure helps them make sense of their world and provides a comforting rhythm to their daily lives. Understanding these sensitive periods allows you to tailor your approach, creating an environment that supports and nurtures your child's natural inclinations.

To identify these sensitive periods, consider keeping a developmental milestones chart. This tool helps you track your child's progress and recognize patterns in their behavior and interests. Maybe you notice your toddler suddenly has a fascination with small objects or is meticulously lining up their toys. These are clues that they are experiencing a sensitive period for order, an opportunity to introduce activities that cater to this developmental stage. Paying attention to changes in behavior, such as a sudden interest in books or an eagerness to help with daily chores, can also signal a shift into a new sensitive period. By being an attentive observer, you can better support your child's growth, adapting your interactions and the environment to align with their evolving needs.

Here is a quick overview of the different sensitive periods. The age periods can vary from child to child, but this will give you a general idea of when to expect those specific developmental phases.

Sensitive Period for Language Acquisition (Birth to Six Years)

In this sensitive period, children's minds are incredibly receptive to words, quickly absorbing vocabulary, sentence structure, and language nuances. They effortlessly soak up words and meanings from their environment, making it a critical time for parents and caregivers to actively support their language development by providing age-appropriate books and having daily reading sessions together. Introduce games and activities that expand vocabulary, like picture books, nursery rhymes, or simple word cards with images. These activities engage your child's natural curiosity and help build their linguistic skills

Sensitive Period for Order and Precision (Two to Four Years)

Between ages two and four, children crave a sense of order and precision. They seek consistency and predictability, desiring a world where everything has its place. This period invites developing a structured environment. Parents can support this by creating an organized space, that fosters tidiness and attention to details. Use baskets or bins to organize toys and label them with pictures or words, helping your child learn the importance of organization. Setting up a daily routine chart can work wonders. Encourage your child to participate in tidying up, transforming it into a game or a shared activity. These practices satisfy their need for structure and empower them to take responsibility for their space.

Sensitive Period for Movement and Coordination (Birth to Five Years)

From crawling to taking their first steps, children are on a quest to refine their motor skills. This phase is marked by an eagerness for movement and coordination, as they discover and hone their physical capabilities. Parents can support this development by creating a safe and engaging environment that encourages the growth of these skills, guiding their children toward becoming confident and adept individuals. Consider having a play area that encourages crawling, jumping, climbing, rolling, dancing, and playing safely.

Sensitive Period for Sensory Exploration (Birth to Five Years)

From birth to five, children are intently exploring the world through their senses. This sensitive period is key for cognitive development, as they are especially attracted to tactile, auditory, and visual stimuli. By offering a variety of sensory experiences—from different textures to nature's sounds—you can significantly enhance their learning and curiosity. Feel free to explore the different sensory exploration activities in the activities list at the end of the book. Creating an environment rich in sensory opportunities fosters their understanding of the world and promotes sensory awareness.

Sensitive Period for Social Development (Two to Four Years)

Between ages two and four, children experience significant social development, showing more interest in peers and developing key social skills. This period is crucial for learning empathy, cooperation, compromise, sharing, and complex social behaviors. Parents can support this by creating opportunities for positive interactions and exemplifying respectful, empathetic behavior. Play dates and regular visits to the park are great settings to hone their social skills while having a ton of fun.

Sensitive periods offer a unique opportunity to connect with your child on a deeper level, understanding and nurturing their natural growth. By recognizing these phases and adjusting your approach, you support their development in a way that feels intuitive and rewarding. Again, the importance of observation cannot be overstated. The more you observe your child attentively, the more you will instinctively know what to provide to take their self-directed exploration to the next level.

Hands-On Learning: Connecting the Neural Dots

Maria Montessori was a firm believer in involving the child into every aspect of daily life activities. Children naturally want to help. They will observe the way parents are doing something and will try to reproduce it to the best of their ability. It is our job to guide them by giving them minimal instructions and letting them do the rest.

> *"The instructions of the teacher consist then merely in a hint, a touch—enough to give a start to the child. The rest develops of itself."*
>
> -Maria Montessori,
> *Dr. Montessori's Own Handbook*

It doesn't have to be verbal instructions; a simple repetition of the movement in a slower manner or by enhancing some part of the movement can often suffice. If you notice your child intensely looking at you while you are sweeping the floor for example, you can repeat your movements slower, then offer them to join you with their own broom.

When children use their hands to act, build, create, or experiment, they connect physical movements with cognitive processes. This active engagement helps embed knowledge in a way that passive learning never can. Painting is great at any age. Babies can experiment painting with their feet and hands on a giant paper, while older children can tackle more precise painting with a brush. Simple wooden cubes are also a timeless classic. By building structures and seeing them crumble, children assimilate basic physics concepts and cause and effect principles. Magnetic building kits are a sure hit with every kid. These creative tactile experiences solidify abstract ideas, making them tangible and easier to grasp.

Encouraging exploration through creative activities can spark curiosity and foster a love for learning. Start with DIY crafts using recyclables. Gather materials like cardboard boxes, fabric scraps, or plastic containers, and watch as these everyday items transform into imaginative projects. In this day and age, it's easy to find great simple crafts ideas online. This encourages creativity and also teaches resourcefulness and environmental awareness. Gardening is another fantastic hands-on activity. As your child plants seeds and watches them grow, they learn about plant life cycles and the importance of nurturing living things. This experience connects them with the soil and nature and instills patience and responsibility. These projects don't require elaborate setups or expensive materials—just a willingness to explore and create together. Such hands-on activities are not only stimulating a multitude of areas of the brain, but they are also opportunities for you to bond with your child, sharing in their discoveries and marvels.

Nature as a Classroom: Incorporating the Outdoors

When you step outside with your child, you open the door to a world teeming with opportunities for growth and discovery. Nature isn't just the backdrop for childhood adventures; it's a rich classroom that offers benefits for both physical and mental well-being. The fresh air and open spaces encourage active play, which is the raw basis for developing coordination and strength. As they run, climb, and explore, children build endurance and physical health. Additionally, the natural environment provides a unique setting that can increase focus and attention. Have you noticed how a walk in the park seems to calm the mind and spark creativity? For children, this effect is magnified. The sensory experiences of rustling leaves, chirping birds, and the scent of flowers engage their senses fully, enhancing their ability to concentrate and observe.

Integrating nature into your child's learning doesn't require elaborate plans. Simple activities like nature scavenger hunts can turn a walk into an educational adventure. Create a list of items to find—a feather, a pine cone, a smooth pebble—and watch as your child eagerly searches for each treasure. This activity sharpens observation skills and encourages curiosity about the natural world. And why not combine those hunts with a follow-up DIY crafts activity at home? Leaves collages or natural objects dipped in paint for imprints on paper make incredibly fun activities for children of all ages. Another engaging idea is to observe weather patterns and changes. Set up a small weather station with a thermometer and rain gauge, and track the daily weather together. Discuss how clouds form or why the wind blows, turning everyday weather into a science lesson. These activities mesh seamlessly with the rhythms of nature, providing learning experiences that are both spontaneous and structured.

Creating nature-based learning spaces at home can further enrich your child's outdoor experiences. Start small by building a garden or herb patch. This hands-on project teaches responsibility and patience as your child tends to the plants and observes their growth. Even a few pots on a windowsill can serve as a mini-garden. Another idea is to create a natural play area in your yard using logs, stones, and sand. These elements encourage imaginative play and exploration, offering a tactile experience that indoor toys often lack. Such spaces allow children to interact with natural materials in an outdoor environment, where your child feels free to explore and learn at their own pace.

Encouraging environmental stewardship is a vital aspect of using nature as a classroom. Simple projects like recycling and composting can introduce your child to sustainable practices. Set up a compost bin together and explain how food scraps turn into nutrient-rich soil. This process teaches about decomposition and highlights the importance of reducing waste. Participating in local clean-up events can further instill a sense of responsibility for the environment. These activities demonstrate the impact one can have in caring for the planet, nurturing a sense of agency in your child. By involving them in these efforts, you cultivate an appreciation for nature and a commitment to preserving it for future generations. Through these experiences, children learn valuable lessons about the interconnectedness of life and their role in maintaining the delicate balance of our ecosystems.

Choosing Developmentally Appropriate Toys

When it comes to choosing toys for your child, it's easy to get swept up in the latest trends and flashy gadgets. But developmentally appropriate toys are the ones that truly support growth and learning. These toys challenge your child's problem-solving abilities and spark creativity. Think about building blocks that help with spatial awareness or puzzles that develop cognitive skills. Such toys encourage exploration and learning through play, allowing your child to experiment and discover on their own terms. By selecting toys that match your child's developmental stage, you provide them with the tools they need to grow and thrive.

Finding the right balance between educational and fun toys can be a challenge, but it's all about offering variety. Look for toys that are not only enjoyable but also beneficial, like interactive books that engage early readers or construction sets that inspire creativity. These toys provide opportunities for learning while keeping playtime exciting and engaging. It's about creating a toy collection that caters to different interests and skills, supporting your child's holistic development.

Avoiding overstimulation is important in maintaining a balanced toy environment. Too many toys can overwhelm your child, making it difficult for them to focus and engage deeply. Have a limited number of toys available to your child, and rotate these toys regularly, taking cues from their interest at the moment. Limit battery-operated toys that often dominate with noise and lights, and instead encourage toys that are open-ended and invite creativity and problem-solving. Also, remember that a cardboard box can become a spaceship or a castle, sparking creativity in ways a pre-programmed toy cannot. By keeping the toy selection simple and intentional, you create a space that fosters imagination and discovery, allowing your child to delve into play with focus and enthusiasm.

Although pretend-play toys like kitchens and plastic tea sets can engage imagination and social play, Montessori favors giving the child the real-life experience. Children's wooden or plastic knives cutting sets, silicone pitchers and cups, bowls and whisks; these are all items that allow children from as early as 18 months of age to start participating in the preparation of meals. Children's broom and mop kits invite their early participation in keeping the house clean. Thinking Montessori means capitalizing on the child's innate desire to contribute to the family's daily tasks. More on this in Chapter 6, where we involve children in every aspect of the daily routines of modern life.

> *"In short, where the manufacture of toys has been brought to a point of such complication and perfection that children have at their disposal entire dolls' houses, complete wardrobes for the dressing and undressing of dolls, kitchens where they can pretend to cook, toy animals as nearly lifelike as possible, this method seeks to give all this to the*

child in reality-making him an actor in a living scene."

-Maria Montessori
Dr. Montessori's Own Handbook

Always prioritize real-life activities and experiences over pretend-play, and keep a deliberate and intentional toy collection that challenges and keeps your child engaged for those free-play sessions.

If you are interested in Maria Montessori's own learning materials for children of various ages, I have put together a list of all her original designs at the end of this book. I suggest you check it out, as I'm sure it will inspire you to create your own collection of toys and learning materials more intentionally.

DIY Montessori Materials: Budget-Friendly Solutions

Imagine your child crafting a toy that perfectly matches their interests—a toy that's not only fun but also tailored to their learning needs. That's the magic of DIY Montessori materials. Creating these items at home offers a level of customization that commercial products simply can't match. Plus, it's a fantastic way to save money. DIY materials can be just as effective, if not more so because you can design them to align perfectly with your child's current developmental stage and interests. Whether it's a set of sensory bottles filled with colorful liquids, homemade play dough scented with essential oils, or personalized sensory boards, these items bring learning to life in a personal and meaningful way.

Let's start with sensory bottles and shakers. These are simple to make and provide endless fascination. Gather a few clear plastic bottles and fill them with various materials—water and glitter, rice and small beads, or even colored oil and water. Seal the lids tightly and let your child shake, roll, and observe the interactions inside. The movement and sound captivate their senses, fostering cognitive development and sensory awareness. Homemade play dough is another fantastic project. Mix flour, salt, water, and a bit of oil, along with food coloring or natural dyes. Let your child mold it, exploring textures and colors. It's not just about the end product; the process itself is a rich learning experience.

Involving your child in creating these materials transforms a simple craft into an educational activity. Encourage them to help with painting and decorating their DIY creations. This not only personalizes the items but also boosts their fine motor skills and creativity. When making play dough, have them measure and mix the ingredients. This hands-on involvement teaches basic math and science concepts, as they measure quantities and see how different components come together to form something new. By engaging them in the creation process, you foster a sense of ownership and pride, making the learning experience even more impactful.

Sensory boards are amazingly fun to build, even if you are not the handy type. Gather locks, switches, gears, bells, door knobs, buttons, and a few scraps of different textured materials like pieces of sand paper, carpet, artificial turf, towel, rubber mat, Lego pieces, velvet, leather, etc. and attach them securely on a wooden board. The sensory experience and problem-solving exploration they provide is sensational. And best of all, no cleanup afterward!

Think creatively about everyday items around your house. You'd be amazed at the Montessori activities you can develop using common household objects. Kitchen utensils, for instance, can become tools for practical life skills. Measuring spoons and cups can teach your child about volume and numbers while engaging them in everyday tasks like cooking. Recycled containers, like egg cartons or cereal boxes, can be transformed into sorting and counting games. Encourage your child to sort buttons by color or size, or use the containers as molds for creative building projects. These activities not only recycle household items but also teach valuable lessons in resourcefulness and sustainability. By repurposing these items, you show your child that learning doesn't require expensive gadgets—just a bit of creativity and imagination.

Finally, remember that Nature provides us with 100% free and beautiful materials that can serve as a starting point for wonderful toy creations and crafts activities. Leaves, pebbles, branches, pine cones, nuts, seeds, sand, rocks, shells, bones, bark, vines, and fir needles are all examples of objects that can both spark creativity and enhance your little one's connection with the natural world. I suggest you check out the Arts and Crafts activities at the end of the book, along with online DIY videos for inspiring ideas.

Next, we delve into how self-directed learning builds upon the absorbent mind, shaping confident, self-motivated individuals.

CHAPTER 3
SELF-DIRECTED LEARNING

"How fascinating it is that every human seems to be born with an inner compass that tells them where to go and what to do at any given moment, and how from the trusting in this compass infallibly emerges passion, purpose, and the mysterious ability to be at the right place at the right time."

- Gabriel Beauchemin

As a parent, stepping back to let your child lead can be challenging. The instinct to guide and protect often pulls us toward oversight. However, as we discussed in chapter 1, the Montessori method emphasizes observation over direction, allowing children the freedom to explore without constant interference. This doesn't mean abandoning guidance altogether, but rather practicing a gentle presence that supports rather than controls. Watching your child solve a problem independently or invent a new game can be hard, especially when you see them struggle, but it's important to resist the urge to intervene prematurely. Instead, offer support from the sidelines, providing encouragement and suggestions only when asked. This approach fosters resilience and confidence, teaching children that they are capable of overcoming challenges through persistence and creativity.

If your toddler is trying to zip their jacket, for example, and you step in after two seconds, they may very well think : "This is too difficult for me, I can't do it." Then it might take a while before they build the confidence to make another attempt. It's important to give them a real chance, even if you believe the task they are taking on is way above their current skill level. Wait for them to ask for help, or to abandon. If they feel discouraged after trying, you might want to reassure them by emphasizing the high difficulty of the task, or by saying that it is hard even for you! In any case, you can always commend their effort and perseverance and encourage them to try again rather than focusing on the result. If they do succeed after struggling for a while, the surge of confidence and joy they will experience from that success will almost make you wish they struggled more often! So make it a habit to step back and leave room for the magic to happen.

Trusting in your child's capabilities is fundamental to promoting self-direction. Believing in their ability to learn independently encourages them to take risks and try new things. Providing opportunities for decision-making can start with small choices, like selecting their clothes for the day or choosing between two snacks. As they grow more confident, these decisions can expand to include planning parts of their daily routine, picking out books to read, or participate in the decoration of their room. When they are old enough, you can certainly go as far as including them in the set-up of certain house rules. Setting up new rules after a conflict arises not only makes it more probable that they will respect the very rules that they themselves participated in creating, but it also engages their critical thinking, problem-solving skills, and ability to anticipate potential problems. This will prove especially effective if they have siblings with whom they can practice these skills with. It will also promote more harmonious ways of interacting socially with any of their peers. Again, it's about giving them the help and tools they need to get started, and then giving them the space to grow on their own.

The balance between guidance and autonomy is delicate yet essential. Offer help only when your child requests it, trusting that they will let you know when they need assistance. Encouraging self-assessment and reflection can be a powerful tool in developing autonomy. After completing a task, you can ask your child how the process went and what they might do differently next time. This reflection encourages critical thinking and self-awareness. Be careful not to overbear them with constant questioning, but do it when it feels natural and between two periods of concentration. By prompting reflections and allowing them the space to evaluate their experiences, you empower them to take charge of their learning experience with more awareness.

Creating a supportive environment at home is integral in facilitating self-directed learning. Organize materials for easy access, ensuring that your child can independently choose and use their resources. Low shelves, labeled bins, and accessible workspaces are just a few ways to design a child-friendly layout. This setup not only promotes independence but also encourages exploration and creativity. A flexible environment adapts to your child's changing interests, offering new challenges as they grow. Consider rotating toys and learning materials to maintain interest and introduce fresh opportunities for discovery.

It's fascinating to see how children's interests emerge and guide them, often leading to unexpected and delightful discoveries. Encouraging exploration of these emerging interests is key to fostering a love of learning. When children choose activities based on what captivates them, they engage more deeply, developing skills and knowledge in ways that feel seamless and enjoyable. Make it a top priority to support your child in their areas of interest throughout their upbringing. Although steering children toward our own personal interests as parents, or what we think is best for them, might be tempting at times, it's vital to trust in their ability to know what they need to learn at any given moment. While we can certainly help them understand the consequences of their choices in the bigger picture, it's important that they feel free to explore their interests for their own sake. That way, we ensure that their love for learning stays strong, and that their future endeavors as adults stay rooted in passion, purpose, and joy.

Creating Individualized Learning Paths: Tailored Approaches

Every child is unique, with their own way of understanding the world. Recognizing your child's learning style can help you nurture their development and confidence.

You might have a visual learner, captivated by pictures and diagrams, who thrives when they see information laid out in a way they can visualize. Or perhaps your child is more auditory, absorbing lessons best through sounds, songs, and verbal instructions. Then there are kinesthetic learners, those little movers and shakers who need to touch and engage physically with their learning materials to fully grasp new concepts. Identifying your child's preferred style can transform their learning experience from a struggle into a joy. Once you know how they learn best, you can adapt activities to suit their strengths. For a visual learner, try incorporating colorful charts or picture books. With auditory learners, focus on storytelling or interactive reading. Kinesthetic kids might benefit from hands-on projects or educational games that get them moving. This tailored approach makes learning more effective and also more enjoyable.

Designing personalized learning experiences goes beyond just recognizing learning styles. It involves setting individualized goals and milestones that reflect your child's interests and abilities. When your child is old enough, discuss with them what they'd like to achieve, whether it's learning a certain language or mastering a new skill. By involving them in the goal-setting process, you empower them to take ownership of their learning. Integrate their interests into educational activities to keep them engaged. A child fascinated by animals might enjoy a project creating a habitat diorama, while one interested in space could build a model of the solar system. These personalized experiences make learning relevant and exciting, tying new knowledge to things they love.

Using flexible teaching methods is key to supporting individualized learning paths. Embrace a variety of activities and resources that cater to different learning styles and interests. This might mean mixing traditional worksheets with interactive apps or combining group projects with solo explorations. Allow for changes in pace and focus, adapting your approach as your child's needs evolve. Some days they may want to dive deep into a topic, while others they might prefer a broader exploration. Flexibility means being responsive and open to shifting gears when necessary. This adaptability ensures that learning remains dynamic and responsive to your child's curiosity and growth. It respects their autonomy while providing the structure needed to guide their educational development.

Tracking progress and adapting plans play a key role in personalizing learning experiences. Regular check-ins and reflections can help you assess what's working and what might need adjustment. Sit down with your child to discuss their progress and experiences. What have they enjoyed? What challenges have they faced? Use these conversations to gather feedback and refine their learning path. Adjust activities based on their input and results, ensuring that they continue to be challenged and engaged. This process keeps learning relevant and fosters a sense of partnership between you and your child. It shows them that their opinions matter and instills confidence in their ability to shape their educational journey. By remaining attentive and adaptable, you create a supportive framework that encourages growth and exploration.

Learning Style Quiz

Take a moment to explore your child's preferred learning style with this simple quiz. Observe them during various activities and note where they seem most engaged and successful:

1. *When learning new information, does your child prefer:*

   a) Watching videos or looking at pictures

   b) Listening to stories or instructions

   c) Engaging in physical activities or experiments

2. *During playtime, do they often:*

   a) Draw or build with blocks

   b) Sing or talk with friends

   c) Run, climb, or move around

3. *In conversations, do they:*

   a) Use descriptive language to paint a picture

   b) Enjoy discussing their thoughts and ideas

   c) Gesture or move while speaking

Reflect on your answers to identify your child's learning style. Use this insight to tailor their learning experiences, creating a path that aligns with their natural inclinations. If many answers come up at once, you can mix and match their learning opportunities and see what works best. If your child is balanced between all learning styles, just keep providing a variety of different styles of learning materials, and let your child choose according to their interest at the moment.

Milestones and Natural Pace: Avoiding Comparison Traps

Every parent has felt that little pang of worry when their child isn't walking, talking, or reading as soon as a neighbor's youngster. It's all too easy to fall into the comparison trap, measuring your child's progress against others. Yet, it's important to remember that children develop at their own pace, each one following a unique timeline. Just as some children sprout up like sunflowers overnight while others grow steadily, individual development varies widely. This natural variation is not merely normal; it's to be expected. Comparing your child to others can lead to unnecessary stress and might even overlook the incredible milestones they are achieving in their own time. Instead, focus on your child's individual path and celebrate their personal journey of growth.

To avoid the pressure of comparisons, consider using developmental checklists as a tool for tracking progress. These checklists provide a broad framework of typical developmental milestones but remember, they are just guides. They can help you understand the general order in which skills emerge without tying you to rigid timelines. Observing your child as they grow is a chance to note the subtle ways they change and adapt. Perhaps your child has developed a knack for storytelling long before mastering the bike. Recognize these achievements as valid and significant. This method of tracking progress keeps the focus on your child's unique strengths and milestones, offering a more personalized perspective on their development.

It's natural to have concerns about whether your child is keeping up with peers. Many parents worry about the implications of not hitting milestones "on time." It's important to address these fears by normalizing the idea that children develop at different rates. The myth of a universal timeline often creates undue pressure, suggesting that all children should reach the same benchmarks simultaneously. In reality, your child's pace is just as valid as any other, and it's vital to honor this individual growth pattern. Each child has their own set of talents and challenges, and recognizing these unique qualities can be more rewarding than simply checking off milestones on a list.

Remember, childhood isn't a race. It's a series of moments that, when strung together, form a unique tapestry of growth and discovery. By focusing on your child's individual path, you allow them to flourish without the weight of comparison. This approach supports their development and strengthens your bond with them, as you learn to appreciate and celebrate the wonderful little person they are becoming.

That being said, it's perfectly fine to seek advice from professionals if you feel the need to. Seeking the opinions of various specialized experts might alleviate worries, or might provide the additional support that the child needs to grow more confident in one or more areas of their development. Just make sure you don't make the child feel like there is something wrong with them, which would undermine their confidence in exploring new things, and would ultimately slow down their development.

Encouraging Intrinsic Motivation: Cultivating Curiosity

Imagine your child, eyes wide with wonder, asking "why" about everything they see. This natural curiosity is the spark that fuels lifelong learning. Encouraging this intrinsic motivation is about fostering a love for learning that isn't dependent on gold stars or rewards. It's about nurturing a desire to know more, to explore the world, and to find joy in the process of discovery itself. You can start by encouraging questioning and exploration in everyday life. When you embrace their endless stream of questions, you invite them to think critically and seek answers. Provide opportunities for self-directed discovery—whether it's a box of old clothes for dress-up or a magnifying glass for backyard explorations. These experiences help children understand that learning is an adventure, one they can lead.

Steering clear of external rewards and pressures is crucial in this process. While it might be tempting to offer praise for achievements, it's more beneficial to recognize their efforts with descriptive feedback. Instead of saying, "Good job," you might mention, "You really worked hard on that puzzle, didn't you? Trying different pieces until you found the right fit. Never giving up. That's how you do it!" This kind of feedback highlights their perseverance and problem-solving skills, encouraging them to value the process over the product. Allowing natural consequences to guide learning is another powerful tool. If a child forgets to water their plant, seeing it wilt teaches responsibility and the impact of their actions. These lessons stick far better than any reprimand or reward.

Creating an environment that inspires curiosity requires a bit of thought and creativity. Curate diverse and engaging materials that vary in texture, color, and function. Think about a bookshelf filled not just with books, but with puzzles, art supplies, and nature collections. Regularly rotating activities can help maintain interest and prevent boredom. This keeps the learning environment dynamic and inviting, encouraging children to explore different materials and ideas. Having a variety of resources at their fingertips allows them to follow their interests, whether they're fascinated by dinosaurs one week and outer space the next. An ever-changing array of activities ensures there's always something new to discover, keeping their curiosity alive and thriving. Just make sure that each object as a clear space of its own so as to avoid chaotic piles of toys and learning materials. This will ensure a more deliberate and effective self-guided education.

Modeling curiosity and enthusiasm yourself can have a profound impact on your child. Share your personal passions and interests with them. If you love painting, let them see you create art and invite them to join. If you're fascinated by gardening, involve them in planting seeds and watching them grow. Your enthusiasm is contagious, and when children see adults around them engaged in learning, they are inspired to do the same. Engaging in learning activities alongside your child strengthens your bond and demonstrates that learning is a shared experience, one that can be fun and fulfilling. Whether it's baking together and discussing the science behind rising dough or taking apart an old radio to see how it works, these shared moments educate and reinforce the idea that learning is an ongoing, exciting part of life.

Rewards have their place in nurturing confidence and motivation in children, but the goal is to gradually phase out tangible rewards in favor of intrinsic motivation. In relation to social life, children need to learn that the main reason why we do certain things is simply because it's the best thing to do, not just for ourselves, but for others as well. For example, it's okay to praise your child for putting their shoes away without being asked, but you just have to make sure that they do it because they understand that having shoes scattered around is unpleasant and dangerous. Otherwise, they might not do it if they don't feel like being praised at the moment. Just remember that rewards can be a powerful positive tool, but that intrinsic motivation should be prioritized and is more effective in the long run.

Observation Techniques

Imagine sitting quietly, watching your child as they play. There's a certain magic in observing without interrupting, letting them lead with their imagination and curiosity. Observation is more than just watching; it's about truly seeing what captures their attention, what makes their eyes light up. This careful observation is key to personalizing their learning experiences. By identifying their interests and strengths, you can tailor activities that align with what they naturally gravitate towards. Maybe you notice your child is fascinated by how things work, indicating an interest in engineering or construction. On the other hand, if they spend hours with crayons and paper, they might have an artistic flair worth nurturing. Noting these interests allows you to provide materials and opportunities that nurture their passions. At the same time, observation helps identify areas for further development. Perhaps they struggle with fine motor skills; this insight allows you to introduce activities that subtly encourage improvement, like threading beads or cutting shapes.

Developing effective observation skills is not an innate talent, but a practiced one. Start by practicing active and attentive watching. This means being present and focused, without the distraction of phones or other tasks. Keeping some attention on your breathing while you observe your child can greatly enhance the experience. Conscious breathing anchors you in the present moment and calms your nervous system down, turning you into a more relaxed and attentive observer.

Observe your child during different activities and settings to get a fuller picture of their preferences and challenges. Record insights and reflections in real-time. Write down or make mental notes about what you notice, such as the types of play they return to or the questions they ask. Over time, these notes become a valuable resource to track patterns and shifts in their interests. This practice trains you to see beyond the surface, understanding the subtleties of their development and how best to support them.

Using these observations to enhance learning is a powerful tool. Once you've identified what captivates your child, adapt the teaching material you provide to align with these interests. If they love exploring nature, plan activities that involve observing, tracking, collecting and identifying objects in natural settings. Providing challenges that match their developmental needs keeps them engaged without overwhelming them. Perhaps they're ready to tackle more complex puzzles or start learning basic cooking skills.

Tailoring activities in this way encourages them to stretch their abilities, fostering growth and confidence.

Collaboration with your child through observation transforms learning into a shared project. Share what you've observed with them, discussing your findings openly. This dialogue invites them to reflect on their experiences, offering feedback on what they enjoyed or found difficult. Encourage self-reflection by asking questions like, "What did you like about building that tower?" or "How did you feel when you completed that puzzle?" This builds their self-awareness and fosters a sense of partnership in their education.

By honing observation techniques, you deepen your connection with your child, understanding them on a more profound level. These insights allow you to craft personalized learning experiences that honor their individuality and promote growth. Observation isn't just about learning what they like; it's about discovering who they are and supporting their journey with empathy and understanding. With these skills in place, you're ready to explore further, embracing the Montessori principles in every aspect of life, as we will see in the upcoming chapters.

CHAPTER 4
HOLISTIC DEVELOPMENT

"In the child is much knowledge, much wisdom. If we do not profit from it, it is only because of neglect on our part to become humble and to see the wonder of this soul and learn what the child can teach."

-Maria Montessori,
The Theosophist

The different areas of the child's development could be seen as different organs in the body, each playing a different role in allowing the child to explore and respond to their environment in their own unique way. Although each organ can be identified and talked about individually, they are not separate from each other at all. The body functions as a perfectly synchronized dance of interconnection and interdependence, of which the depth and complexity is still, in large part, a mystery. The good news is we don't have to know everything about every aspect of our child's development to nurture their growth in a healthy way.

From the moment children first open their eyes, their tiny body is already equipped with a natural guiding system that is attuned to their needs. As children grow older, this system of self-direction serves as a guide, steering them toward their preferences and areas of interest. It is the recognition of this innate ability that gave birth to Montessori's fundamental principle of *self-directed learning*. Through observation and interaction, children are naturally drawn to activities that match their developmental stage and interests. This self-guided exploration is supported by the child's awareness of their needs and the world around them, focusing on tasks that nurture their growth. By trusting in the child's capacity to determine their educational path, the Montessori method fosters a deeply personal and empowering experience, enabling each child to unlock their potential authentically and wholly. Our role as parents and teachers then becomes one of responding to the child's cues, providing them with the space to engage in experiences that resonate with their evolving needs. In doing so, we honor the child's wisdom and innate drive for growth, ensuring a learning experience that is both enriching and fulfilling in all aspects of their life.

In this chapter, we'll take a look at each area of the child's development, and gain some perspective on how they can be supported in accordance with the method.

Cognitive Development

Picture this: it's a quiet Saturday morning, and you watch your child as they eagerly piece together a puzzle on the living room floor. Their brow furrows in concentration, a subtle smile on their face as they click the final piece into place. This scene of focused engagement is a window into the vast world of cognitive growth. In our fast-paced lives, it can be easy to overlook these small moments. Yet, they are the building blocks of a child's ability to think critically and creatively. Cognitive growth is about nurturing young minds to explore, question, and learn by doing.

When we use the word *cognitive*, we refer to anything related to the mental processes involved in gaining knowledge and understanding. These processes include thinking, learning, memory, problem-solving, perception, attention, reasoning, and language. In essence, cognitive functions are how the brain processes information to make sense of the world and guide behavior. This process is active at all times, and it allows the child to evolve and make new choices based on the new information gained every moment. In early childhood, children primarily learn through their senses, absorbing information that helps them grasp the tangible aspects of their environment. This sensorial exploration lays the groundwork for understanding the physical world. As they grow and master these foundational concepts, their innate curiosity propels them toward language acquisition. This progression from sensory-based learning to linguistic development enables children to further explore and make sense of their surroundings.

Language opens many doors; it lets you refer to objects and events that are not here right now, and things that may be present but are not as tangible, like the feeling of fatigue, or the need to go to the bathroom. Through language, children are able to communicate their needs more clearly, which allows parents to better support them in return. Once the ability of the child reaches a certain level, they start inquiring about the world by taking advantage of the knowledge of the parents. This means that they ask a lot of questions, about a lot of things.

Although it can be tiring to answer a million questions a day, embracing the child's curiosity is key. When they wonder why the sky is blue or how plants grow, engage with them. Try exploring these questions together, perhaps by looking up answers in books or observing nature. Providing a variety of stimulating materials can also ignite their curiosity and partially alleviate your job to explain everything. Fill your home with diverse resources like books, toys, and educational games that invite exploration. These materials are both tools for learning and invitations to discover new interests and ideas. Surrounding your child with opportunities to explore will cultivate a mindset of curiosity and wonder.

As your child grows, introducing age-appropriate cognitive challenges helps them develop essential skills. Puzzles and logic games are fantastic for developing problem-solving abilities and critical thinking. They encourage your child to think strategically, testing different solutions until they find one that works. Memory and sequencing tasks, like matching games or storytelling exercises, sharpen focus and cognitive flexibility. These activities engage their minds, offering challenges that are just tough enough to push them forward without causing frustration. Tailor these challenges to your child's developmental stage, ensuring they remain engaging and rewarding.

Montessori materials are invaluable in supporting cognitive development. Crafted by Maria Montessori herself to stimulate specific functions of the brain, these tools remain relevant today. Consider tools like the pink tower or number rods, which offer hands-on learning experiences that enhance understanding. The pink tower, for example, consists of ten wooden cubes that vary in size, teaching concepts of dimension and volume through manipulation. Demonstrate how to use these materials, showing your child how to stack the cubes or arrange the rods. Encourage them to explore different configurations and observe the relationships between the pieces. Original Montessori learning materials make a great addition to any play area. Again, I invite you to check out the complete list of the original Montessori learning materials I have put together at the end of this book.

Physical Development: Building Strength and Coordination

Imagine the sheer joy on your child's face as they run across the yard, arms wide, chasing the wind. These moments of outdoor play are the celebration of the outside world, and are essential for physical development. There is no equal to regular outdoor play and exploration for promoting health and fitness. Let your child climb trees, roll down hills, and dig in the dirt. These activities build strength and endurance, letting them stretch their muscles and imagination and engage their sensory functions in a hands-on manner. Encourage them to explore different terrains, like sand, grass, and gravel, each offering unique challenges and sensations.

Structured activities like yoga or dance provide another layer of physical development. Both offer a blend of movement and focus, teaching balance, flexibility, and coordination. Yoga, with its gentle stretches and poses, encourages mindfulness and body awareness. Introduce your child to simple poses like the tree or cat-cow, guiding them through breathing and movement. Dance, on the other hand, allows for self-expression and creativity. Whether it's twirling to a favorite song or learning a choreographed routine, dance improves rhythm and coordination. These structured activities complement free play, offering a balanced approach to fitness. Mix structured and unstructured activities to create a fitness routine that supports overall well-being.

Developing fine and gross motor skills is an ongoing process that can be both fun and rewarding. Fine motor skills involve smaller muscle movements, which are crucial for tasks like writing and buttoning clothes. Activities like threading beads or using lacing cards strengthen these muscles, improving dexterity and hand-eye coordination. Provide a variety of materials—different-sized beads, colorful laces, and interesting shapes—to keep the activities engaging. Gross motor skills, involving larger muscle movements, are equally important. Encouraging your child to climb and balance can enhance their physical abilities. Set up a simple obstacle course with pillows to jump over, or a balance beam made from a sturdy plank. These exercises build strength, improve balance, and increase confidence as your child masters new challenges.

Hand-eye coordination is another important aspect of physical development. Ball games are a fantastic way to refine these skills. Playing catch, for instance, requires your child to track the ball with their eyes while coordinating their hands to catch it. Start with a soft ball and gradually increase the difficulty as they improve. With younger children, simply sit face to face and roll the ball toward each other. Building and stacking activities also boost hand-eye coordination. Provide blocks or stacking cups, encouraging your child to create towers or patterns. These activities require precision and patience, teaching them to focus and adjust their movements. As they practice, you'll notice improvements in their ability to coordinate their actions.

For toddlers, simple obstacle courses can provide safe yet stimulating fun. Use everyday objects like cushions, chairs, and blankets to create tunnels and hurdles. These courses encourage crawling, climbing, and balancing, building strength and coordination in a playful setting. As children grow, introduce more complex activities that match their increased abilities and interests. Whether it's soccer, gymnastics, or martial arts, these activities offer structured environments where they can further develop their skills. Encourage them to try different sports, discovering what they enjoy most. Regular visits to a park with play structures for children is also strongly encouraged.

Language and Communication Skills

Maria Montessori believed that language skills are acquired naturally as children engage in a prepared, language-rich environment that supports their innate drive to communicate. In the Montessori method, language development begins indirectly, with sensorial and motor activities that strengthen concentration, order, and fine motor control—essential for writing. Materials like sandpaper letters, movable alphabets, and practical life activities encourage phonetic awareness and letter formation, helping children connect sounds with symbols.

Hang clear, simple language materials on the walls, so that the child may absorb knowledge both consciously and unconsciously. A constant exposure to such information helps internalize the basics and make the learning of reading and writing easier when they start putting the words together intentionally. Have an intentional collection of age-appropriate books on an accessible shelf and a small, comfortable reading corner if the space allows for it.

Spoken language develops first through immersion, with adults modeling clear, rich language. As children gain vocabulary and phonetic understanding, they progress to reading and writing, often spontaneously, as they are ready. Engaging in regular, meaningful conversations with your child strengthens your bond and boosts their confidence. Employing simple, clear language suited to your child's developmental stage makes communication more effective and accessible.

Bedtime stories are also great for bonding and easy to incorporate into the daily routine, making sure you have at least one shared session of language-oriented activity every day. Ask your child questions during the story to make it more engaging for them. You can ask them to name objects and animals to enhance vocabulary. You can also discuss how the characters are doing and feeling, or how your child is feeling about a particular subject addressed in the book.

As you set-up your home, remember that Montessori environments are designed to encourage independence and confidence, allowing children to explore and refine language skills at their own pace in an engaging, supportive setting.

Practical Life Skills: Everyday Learning Opportunities

Practical life skills are at the core of Montessori teachings, and the reason is simple; they nurture almost every aspect of the child's developmental needs. Through the variety of chores and activities tied to the management of the household, children grow up as independent, confident and resourceful individuals who know how to take care of themselves and others around them. Children naturally want to help. They want to feel like full-fledged members of the family. It's essential to guide this natural inclination in a manner that fosters a child's positive association with chores, enabling them to embrace the myriad benefits these tasks provide for their development.

Imagine the simple act of setting the table. It may seem mundane, but to a child, it's a lesson in organization, sequencing, and responsibility in which they gladly put a 100% of their concentration. And as Maria Montessori puts it: "The child who concentrates is immensely happy."

As they place each item in its proper spot, they learn about order and precision. Cleaning up after meals offers similar benefits, teaching them about tidiness and cooperation. Filling and emptying the dishwasher machine is very fun and engaging as well. These tasks are more than just routines; they are stepping stones to independence. Incorporating practical life skills into your child's daily schedule not only boosts their confidence but also instills a sense of belonging and contribution. When children participate in household tasks, they feel valued and competent.

Dressing and personal hygiene routines provide another avenue for learning and growth. Encourage your child to dress themselves, starting with simple tasks like pulling on rain boots or buttoning shirts. Over time, these actions build fine motor skills and dexterity. Personal hygiene, such as brushing teeth or washing hands, teaches them about health and self-care. These routines foster independence, empowering children to manage their own needs. As they master these tasks, they gain a sense of pride and accomplishment. Encouraging self-initiated tasks, like choosing their clothes or preparing a simple snack, further enhances their decision-making abilities.

Responsibility and independence are nurtured through age-appropriate chores. Assigning tasks that match your child's abilities promotes self-reliance and accountability. Younger children might enjoy sorting laundry or feeding a pet, while older ones can take on more complex responsibilities like vacuuming or preparing a salad.

Caring for the environment is another vital aspect of practical life skills. Activities like watering plants and tending to a garden teach children about nature and stewardship. As they watch their plants grow, they learn about responsibility and the impact of their actions. Recycling and waste management practices foster environmental awareness, teaching them about sustainability and conservation. Involve your child in sorting recyclables or creating a compost bin, explaining the importance of reducing waste. These activities cultivate a sense of responsibility for the planet, encouraging them to become conscientious citizens. By connecting daily routines with environmental care, you instill values that extend beyond the home.

Montessori materials offer practical tools to develop these life skills. Pouring and spooning exercises, for instance, teach precision and control. Provide small pitchers and bowls for your child to practice pouring water or scooping rice. These activities refine their motor skills and hand-eye coordination, preparing them for more complex tasks. Buttoning and zipping frames are excellent for teaching dressing skills, allowing children to practice in a controlled setting. These frames simulate real-life clothing, helping them master buttons, snaps, and zippers. Through these hands-on activities, children develop confidence and competence.

In chapter 6, we will take a look at how to build our different routines of the day, emphasizing on the child's participation in the different tasks at hand. You will also find more practical life skills activities in the activities list at the end of the book.

Emotional Development: Building Emotional Intelligence and Resilience

As you watch your child grow, you see them encounter a range of emotions—joy, frustration, curiosity, and even anger. Helping children understand and articulate these feelings is crucial for their emotional development. One method to facilitate this is through the use of emotion cards and storytelling. By providing cards with different facial expressions, you can encourage your child to identify and express their emotions in a tangible way. Pair these cards with stories that explore various emotional landscapes. When a story character feels scared, ask your child if they've ever felt the same. This helps them articulate their feelings and builds a vocabulary around emotions, making it easier for them to communicate how they feel. Encouraging verbal expression of emotions turns these moments into discussions, where feelings are validated and understood.

Empathy is the bridge that connects us to others, allowing us to understand and share in their emotions. Developing empathy in children is a gradual process that can be nurtured through activities that promote perspective-taking. Role-playing different scenarios is one such activity. Create situations where your child can "walk in someone else's shoes," perhaps pretending to be a friend who's feeling left out. Discussing characters' emotions in stories is another valuable tool. As you read together, pause to ask your child how they think a character feels and why. These discussions teach them to consider viewpoints outside their own, helping them understand others' experiences and emotions. By regularly engaging in these activities, you help your child develop a deeper sense of empathy and connection to those around them.

Children aren't born with the ability to manage their emotions; it's a skill they learn over time. Teaching emotional regulation involves providing them with strategies to calm and center themselves. Deep breathing and mindfulness exercises are effective techniques for helping children manage emotions. Guide your child to take slow, deep breaths when they're upset, counting to five as they inhale and exhale. This practice helps them focus and regain control. Creating a calming corner or safe space in your home can also offer comfort. Fill this area with soft cushions, favorite books, a plushie, or calming objects. When emotions run high, respectfully encourage your child to retreat to this space, teaching them to self-soothe and process their feelings in a healthy way. These strategies empower them to navigate their emotions in a healthy way.

Life presents challenges—some big, some small—and building resilience equips children to handle these hurdles with confidence. Problem-solving discussions are an excellent way to instill these skills. When faced with a challenge, involve your child in brainstorming solutions. Ask them what they think might work and why, guiding them to evaluate their options and make decisions. Celebrating effort and persistence, rather than just the outcome, reinforces the value of perseverance. Acknowledge the hard work and determination they display, even if the result isn't perfect. This approach teaches them that setbacks are part of learning and that their efforts are always worthwhile. Fostering resilience and coping skills help your child develop the confidence to face adversity and the flexibility to adapt to change. Through these experiences, they learn that they can find solutions and overcome obstacles, transforming challenges into opportunities for growth.

Social Skills: Cultivating Respectful Interactions

Imagine your child in the midst of a lively playdate, surrounded by friends, each one eager to share their story. This scene is a beautiful opportunity to teach effective communication, a skill that forms the foundation of respectful interactions. Encouraging children to communicate effectively starts with practicing active listening. Show them how to give their full attention, making eye contact and nodding to show understanding. Encourage them to listen without interrupting, waiting for their turn to speak. This teaches respect and helps them understand that everyone's voice matters. Alongside listening, promote the use of polite language. Simple phrases like "please" and "thank you" can go a long way in fostering kindness and easing connection. Remind them that words have power and that choosing them wisely can strengthen friendships. Encourage them to greet their friends, offer snacks, and share toys. By modeling these behaviors yourself, you create a home environment where respectful communication is the norm.

Fostering cooperation and teamwork is another vital aspect of social development. Group projects and collaborative games are fantastic ways to teach these skills. They encourage children to work together, share ideas, and learn the value of collective effort. Whether it's building a fort or completing a puzzle, these activities require negotiation and cooperation. Family meetings also offer a platform for teamwork, where everyone can contribute to decision-making. Involve your child in planning family activities or meals, allowing them to voice their opinions and listen to others. This teaches them about compromise and collaboration, preparing them for future interactions in diverse settings. When you integrate teamwork into daily life, you lay the groundwork for strong social bonds and a cooperative spirit.

Conflict is an inevitable part of social interactions, but teaching children to resolve conflicts peacefully is an incredibly valuable skill for building a future generation of strong individuals who are capable of working together. Introduce conflict resolution strategies through games and discussions. Teach them to use negotiation and compromise to find solutions that satisfy everyone involved.

Role-playing conflict scenarios can be particularly effective if you want to teach this skill without having to deal with an intense emotional charge at the same time. Create situations where your child can practice resolving disagreements, guiding them to use words instead of actions. Discuss the importance of understanding each other's perspectives and finding common ground. This helps them manage conflicts and also enhances their empathy and problem-solving abilities.

Modeling social interactions is perhaps one of the most influential ways to teach children about respect and kindness. Children learn by watching the adults in their lives, so demonstrate kindness and empathy in your daily interactions. Whether it's offering a helping hand to a neighbor or listening patiently to a friend, these actions speak volumes. If you are living with a partner, the way you interact with each other will serve as the most powerful example to your child. If you think this area of your life needs improvement, it's time to step up your game, both for the child's sake and your own. Use the love you have for your children as motivation to be the best communicator you know you can be.

You can also encourage inclusive play by inviting children of diverse backgrounds, ages, and abilities to join in activities. Show them the joy of forming connections across differences, emphasizing that everyone has something valuable to contribute. By modeling these behaviors, you inspire your child to embrace diversity and approach social interactions with an open heart and mind. This modeling creates a ripple effect, influencing their friends and peers, and fostering a more inclusive and understanding community. In this way, social skills become not just a part of education, but a valuable contribution to a more compassionate and harmonious society.

Problem-Solving Abilities: Encouraging Critical Thinking

Imagine your child pausing to ponder a question you just asked, a look of curiosity in their eyes. This moment is when the little hamster of critical thinking is exercising his muscles. Encouraging this ability involves posing open-ended questions that don't have a single right answer. Ask them, "What do you think would happen if we mixed these two colors?" or "How could we build a tower that doesn't fall?" These questions invite reflection, exploration, and experimentation, pushing them to think deeply and creatively. When nurturing an environment where questioning is welcomed, you help them learn to analyze situations and consider multiple possibilities. This approach sharpens their analytical skills and also creates a mindset of curiosity and innovation.

Games can be a powerful tool in enhancing problem-solving abilities. Strategy board games, like chess or checkers, require planning and foresight, teaching children to anticipate outcomes and adapt their strategies. Similarly, brain teasers and logic puzzles challenge them to think outside the box, applying logic and reasoning to find solutions. These activities engage their minds, turning problem-solving into a fun and rewarding experience. They learn to break down complex problems into manageable parts, developing perseverance and patience along the way. By incorporating games as a regular part of their routine, you provide opportunities for them to practice these skills in an enjoyable and interactive way.

Incorporating real-world problem-solving opportunities into daily life can further strengthen these skills. Involve your child in planning family activities, like a trip to the park or a weekend picnic. Let them help decide what to pack, considering weather, food preferences, and activities. This task teaches them to weigh options and make decisions, understanding the impact of their choices. Encourage them to take on DIY projects that require planning and execution, such as building a birdhouse or creating a small garden. These projects require them to think critically, plan steps, and adapt to challenges. Real-world experiences offer rich opportunities for learning, allowing them to apply their problem-solving skills in meaningful contexts. They learn that mistakes are part of the process, teaching them resilience and adaptability.

Teaching perseverance and resilience is essential in developing a determined mindset. Celebrate effort and learning from mistakes, reinforcing the idea that setbacks are stepping stones to success. When your child encounters a challenge, focus on the effort they put in rather than the outcome. Praise their determination and creativity, helping them understand that persistence is key to overcoming obstacles. Set challenging yet achievable goals that stretch their abilities without overwhelming them. These goals provide direction and motivation, encouraging them to push their limits and discover their potential.

Math and Numeracy: Unlocking the Secret Code

"Mathematics is the language in which God has written the Universe."

- Galileo

Since young children naturally seek to explore and comprehend their surroundings, mathematics emerges as a fascinating "secret code" that unlocks a deeper understanding of the world around them. Montessori math materials are designed to help them grasp abstract mathematical concepts in a tangible way, allowing children to discover mathematical relationships through hands-on activities and self-directed learning.

The Montessori method emphasizes a progression from concrete to abstract learning. Children first engage with materials that involve physical counting, sorting, and arranging, such as number rods, sandpaper numerals, bead chains, and geometric shape insets. These tools help them develop foundational skills, like one-to-one correspondence, quantity recognition, basic operations (addition, subtraction, multiplication, and division), and geometry by physically manipulating objects. As children's confidence and understanding grow, they naturally progress to more abstract mathematical challenges.

Again, we put the emphasis on creating an environment where age-appropriate materials are accessible to the child whenever they feel the urge to explore these concepts. Displaying posters featuring numbers, basic mathematical operations, and geometric shapes in your child's environment significantly enhances their ability to swiftly and effortlessly internalize these fundamental concepts.

Cooking activities are a great way to engage their math skills. Include the child in counting and measuring the quantities of ingredients needed for a recipe. You can ask them for "'two more dried raisins please" or to "make three more circles with the spoon". If your child is older, you can ask them to "only put one third of the sugar" or to "adjust all the quantities for a double recipe". Be careful not to drown your child in endless questions and challenges, or they might lose interest in the activity. Consider these questions as gentle enhancements to the activity, similar to sprinkling chocolate chips into the cookie dough — enough to enrich the experience without overwhelming it.

Botany and Zoology: Cultivating Relationships With the Living

Tending to the needs of plants and pets at home is perfectly aligned with the method. Assuming responsibility for the care of living things fosters empathy and compassion, enriching their bond with nature. Interacting with animals encourages children to think creatively to ensure activities are enjoyable for both. Meanwhile, nurturing plants demands careful attention and gentle handling, honing their fine motor skills and patience.

Nature walks are an excellent way to cultivate a child's curiosity about the natural environment. On these walks, make it a point to remain observant and guide the child's attention toward the unique plants, mushrooms, and animals you come across. Emphasize the journey rather than the destination, allowing the child to gather as many wonderful and remarkable experiences as possible.

At home, you can extend these nature walks by creating a "nature observation station" where children can display their discoveries. This might include pressed leaves, flower petals, or sketches of animals they've seen. Providing tools like magnifying glasses, small jars, or identification guides allows children to closely examine their finds, deepening their understanding of the natural world. This activity can be paired with nature journaling, where children can record their observations through drawings, descriptions, and questions, cultivating both their artistic and scientific skills.

For younger children, introducing botany and zoology through hands-on care is a perfect fit. Planting a small garden with herbs, flowers, or vegetables gives children the chance to observe the plant life cycle from seed to harvest. Activities like watering, weeding, or harvesting provide a sense of responsibility and accomplishment. For zoology, a small pet such as a fish or hamster can help children learn about the needs of animals, from feeding and cleaning to observing behaviors. In the Montessori classroom, children often work with classified picture cards to explore different plant and animal groups, which can be easily replicated at home using homemade or printable materials.

Older children can take their study of botany and zoology further by exploring ecosystems and interdependence. For example, they might research pollination and its role in plant reproduction, pairing this with activities like building a bee house or planting pollinator-friendly flowers. Zoology lessons could expand into studying animal habitats or food chains, creating dioramas to represent ecosystems, or building bird feeders and observing visiting species. Such activities encourage children to see the interconnectedness of life on Earth and inspire respect for the living world.

Geography and Cosmology: Broadening the Definition of "Home"

> *"I am not an Athenian or a Greek, but a citizen of the world."*
>
> - Socrates

In the Montessori method, geography and cosmology are taught to help children understand their place in the universe and how everything is interconnected. This begins with concrete, hands-on activities that introduce the physical features of Earth and gradually expands to include cultural, historical, and cosmic perspectives. Through these lessons, children develop a sense of belonging to a global and universal community, fostering curiosity, empathy, and environmental awareness. By tailoring activities to each developmental stage, Montessori teachers and parents create an inspiring progression of learning that spans from the tactile exploration of landforms to the vastness of the cosmos.

For younger children, aged 3 to 6, geography lessons focus on tangible, sensory-rich materials. For example, they begin with a sandpaper globe to distinguish land from water by touch. Puzzle maps are introduced to help children learn the shapes and locations of continents, countries, and oceans. Land and water forms, such as islands and lakes, are explored using models that children can pour water into to observe their shapes. At this stage, children are also introduced to cultural geography through continent boxes, which contain items like photographs, small artifacts, and books showcasing the traditions, clothing, and animals of different regions. These activities foster spatial awareness and an appreciation of global diversity while making geography accessible and engaging.

As children move into the elementary years, they begin exploring the relationship between geography and human life, delving into both physical and cultural geography. For instance, they might study how rivers shaped the development of ancient civilizations or how mountains affect climate. Map-making becomes a central activity; children label, draw, and create maps of continents and countries, gradually building skills to interpret geographical data. The Montessori Great Lessons, a series of interconnected stories, introduce cosmology by explaining the formation of the universe, the Earth, and the evolution of life. Experiments demonstrating concepts like erosion, volcano formation, or the water cycle provide a hands-on understanding of Earth's processes and their influence on life.

In the later elementary years and beyond, lessons become increasingly abstract and inquiry-driven. Students explore global issues such as climate change, resource distribution, and cultural exchange, connecting their studies to current events. They might conduct research projects on specific regions, studying their geography, history, and culture in depth. Cosmology lessons extend to the study of astronomy, where students learn about the solar system, stars, and galaxies. Activities could include building scale models of the solar system, observing celestial bodies with telescopes, or conducting experiments about gravity and light. These lessons inspire awe and a deeper understanding of humanity's place in the universe.

The Montessori method's integrated approach to geography and cosmology ensures that children develop a holistic understanding of the world and their role in it. By combining sensory exploration, storytelling, scientific inquiry, and creative projects, children gain not only factual knowledge but also a sense of wonder and responsibility. This progression of learning helps children see the Earth as their home and the universe as their extended neighborhood, instilling a sense of global and cosmic citizenship that aligns with Socrates' timeless insight.

CHAPTER 5
SETTING UP YOUR HOME

Imagine waking up to a peaceful home atmosphere, where everything has its place, and where your child moves confidently from one activity to the next, fueled by curiosity and joy. This is the promise and potential of a Montessori-inspired environment. As parents, we often dream of such order, but struggle to achieve it amidst the chaos of everyday life. Yet, the key lies in creating a *prepared environment*, a concept from which the Montessori philosophy draws its efficacy. This environment is not just about organizing toys but designing spaces that support independence and learning. It shifts the focus from merely keeping children entertained to nurturing their natural abilities and interests. In this chapter, we will look at each room of the house, and see how we can create a safe structure where your child can freely explore and flourish.

The Bedroom

Furniture and Layout

1. Low Bed

- A floor bed or a mattress on a low frame that the child can easily get in and out of independently.

2. Child-Sized Furniture

- A small table and chair for activities like drawing or reading.
- A low shelf for books, toys, and other items.

3. Accessible Storage

- Low drawers or baskets for clothes, allowing the child to dress themselves.
- Hooks at the child's height for jackets, hats, or bags.

4. Soft Lighting

- A small lamp or nightlight within reach to encourage the child to control their environment.

Bedding and Décor

5. Simple Bedding

- A soft, washable blanket or comforter and a small pillow.

6. Child-Friendly Décor

- Artwork hung at the child's eye level.
- Photos, mirrors, or nature prints to make the space welcoming and personal.

7. Rug or Mat

- A soft area rug or mat for sitting, playing, or reading.

Organization and Order

8. Toy Rotation

- A system of rotating toys to prevent clutter and maintain interest.

9. Storage Baskets or Boxes

- Clearly labeled containers for different types of toys or materials.

10. Clothing System

- A small wardrobe or clothing rack where a child can select their outfits.
- Use limited options to avoid overwhelming them.

Learning and Exploration

11. Books

- A small bookshelf with a curated selection of age-appropriate books, rotated regularly.

12. Quiet Area

- A cozy reading corner with cushions, a bean bag, or a small tent.

13. Montessori Materials

- Age-appropriate puzzles, stacking toys, or manipulatives like wooden blocks.

- Practical life activities like threading beads or simple sewing kits.

Personal Care and Responsibility

14. Mirror at Child's Height

- A safe, shatterproof mirror for self-care activities like brushing hair.

15. Laundry Basket

- A small basket for the child to collect their dirty clothes.

16. Trash Bin

- A child-sized trash bin to encourage tidiness.

Comfort and Calm

17. Natural Elements

- A small plant for the child to care for or nature-inspired decorations.

18. Music and Relaxation

- A child-friendly music player or sound machine for calming music or nature sounds.

19. Personal Items

- A special shelf or box for treasures, photos, or sentimental items.

The Kitchen

Furniture and Setup

1. **Child-Sized Furniture**
   - A small table and chair for eating or food prep.
   - A step stool or Montessori learning tower to safely reach counters and work comfortably.

2. **Accessible Shelves or Drawers**
   - Set up a low drawer or cabinet for utensils, plates, and food items.

3. **Child-Friendly Workspace**
   - A designated area for the child to work, such as a low counter or a tray for specific tasks.

Child-Sized Tools

4. **Utensils**
   - Small spoons, forks, and butter knives (blunt, child-safe).
   - A whisk, tongs, and spatulas.

5. **Food Prep Tools**
   - A child-sized cutting board and a small wooden or plastic knife.
   - A hand juicer, mini rolling pin, and cookie cutters.
   - A child-safe grater for cheese or vegetables.

6. **Measuring Tools**

- Small measuring cups and spoons.
- A small mixing bowl with a rubber base to prevent slipping.

Serving and Cleaning

7. Dishes and Utensils

- Unbreakable but real plates, bowls, and cups (e.g., silicone, bamboo, stainless steel, or tempered glass).
- A small pitcher for pouring water or juice.

8. Cleaning Supplies

- A small broom, dustpan, and mop.
- A child-sized sponge, dishcloth, or scrub brush.
- A small bucket for carrying water or cleaning spills.

Food Storage and Access

9. Snack Station

- A basket or tray with pre-portioned healthy snacks like fruit, crackers, or nuts.
- A mini fridge or a low shelf in the main fridge for child-accessible items like yogurt or cut veggies.

10. Containers

- Small, easy-to-open containers for storing leftovers or snacks.

Learning and Fun

11. Recipe Cards

- Simple, illustrated recipe cards for the child to follow independently.

12. Gardening Connection

- Small potted herbs (like basil or mint) to connect food prep with plant care.

13. Timers

- A child-friendly timer to help them learn about time in cooking tasks.

The Play Area

Furniture and Layout

1. Low Shelves

- Open, child-height shelves to display toys and materials neatly.

2. Child-Sized Table and Chairs

- A small table for activities like drawing, puzzles, or practical life tasks.

3. Comfortable Floor Space

- A soft rug or mat for building, playing, or relaxing.

4. Defined Activity Areas

- If possible, separate spaces for specific activities, such as art, construction, climbing, or reading.

Toys and Materials (refer to the list of Montessori didactic materials for additional ideas)

5. Open-Ended Toys

- Wooden blocks, stacking toys, or magnetic tiles to encourage creativity and problem-solving.
- A bin with natural materials like stones, shells, or pine cones for sensory exploration.

6. Puzzles and Games

- Age-appropriate puzzles with varying difficulty levels.
- Simple matching or memory games.

7. Role-Play Items

- Costumes or dress-up clothes to foster imaginative play.

8. Sensory Boards and Walls

- Have an engaging sensory board with buttons, switches, locks, gears, and other interactive elements.
- Hang up different scraps of textured materials on the wall like sandpaper, rubber, bubble wrap, velvet, or artificial turf for sensory exploration.

Art and Creativity

9. Art Supplies

- Washable crayons, markers, colored pencils, and paints.

- Paper, scissors (child-safe), glue, and stickers for crafting.

10. Easel or Drawing Board

- A small easel or chalkboard for drawing and writing.

11. Display Area

- A board or wall space to showcase the child's artwork.

Books and Reading

12. Book Display

- A low bookshelf or a forward-facing book rack to make books easily accessible.

13. Cozy Reading Nook

- Cushions, a beanbag chair, or a soft mat in a quiet corner for reading.

Gross Motor Activities

14. Climbing and Movement

- A Pikler triangle, balance beam, or stepping stones for safe physical play.
- Small, low climbing panels mounted securely for indoor exploration. (place a mattress at the base for safety)
- A wobble or rocker board to develop core strength and balance.

15. Movement Props

- A basket with scarves, ribbons, or a soft ball for active play.

16. Music and Dance

- Percussion instruments like maracas, tambourines, a small piano, or a xylophone.
- A child-friendly music player for dance and movement activities.

Organization and Storage

17. Low shelf or cube storage

- Low-shelves or cube storage where every object has its own designated place.
- Rotate toys regularly to keep the space fresh and engaging.

18. Baskets or Trays

- Containers for grouping similar materials or activities.

19. Clear Labels or Photos

- Use visual labels to help the child return items to their proper place.

20. Work Mats

- A large rug or mat to define the workspace for activities.

Natural and Calming Elements

21. Plants

- Small, non-toxic plants that the child can help care for.

22. Natural Light

- Position the play area near a window for natural light.

23. Calming Décor

- Use neutral colors and minimal decorations with natural materials to create a peaceful environment.

The Bathroom

Accessible Fixtures and Furniture

1. Step Stool

- A sturdy, non-slip stool to help the child reach the sink, toilet, and other fixtures.

2. Child-Sized Potty or Seat

- A child potty or a secure toilet seat adapter to encourage independent toileting.

3. Low Hooks or Towel Bars

- Install hooks or bars at the child's height for towels, washcloths, and robes.

4. Mirror at Child's Height

- A safe, shatterproof mirror for self-care activities like brushing teeth and washing their face.

Personal Care Items

5. Toothbrushing Setup

- A child-sized toothbrush and toothpaste placed in a small cup or holder within easy reach.

6. Handwashing Station

- A pump soap dispenser that's easy for little hands to operate.
- A small towel or washcloth nearby for drying hands.

7. Hair Care Items

- A child-sized brush or comb stored within reach.
- A small spray bottle of water for taming hair if needed.

Bath Time

8. Bath Supplies

- Mild, child-friendly soap and shampoo in easy-to-use pump bottles.
- A small sponge or washcloth for the child to wash themselves.

9. Bath Toys and Storage

- Simple toys like cups, boats, or animals for sensory play, stored in a mesh bag or basket for easy drying.

10. Non-Slip Mat

- A safety mat in the tub or shower to prevent slipping.

Toileting Independence

11. Toilet Paper Holder

- Install a low toilet paper holder so the child can access and use it independently.

12. Flush Handle Extender

- An extender or an easy-to-reach lever to encourage independent flushing.

13. Small Trash Can

- A child-sized trash bin for used tissues or wipes.

Organization and Storage

14. Low Shelves, Baskets, or Drawers

- Store toiletries and towels in accessible containers, baskets or drawers at the child's height.

15. Labeled Containers

- Use clear labels or pictures for organizing items like toothbrushes, soap, and bath toys.

16. Laundry Basket

- A small, child-friendly laundry basket to encourage responsibility for dirty clothes and towels.

Hygiene Practices

17. Handwashing Reminder Chart

- A visual step-by-step guide for washing hands or brushing teeth.

18. Tissue Box

- A small box of tissues within reach to promote good hygiene habits.

19. Nail Care

- A small, rounded nail brush for cleaning under nails.

Comfort and Safety

20. Soft Towels and Rugs

- Plush, absorbent towels and a non-slip rug for warmth and safety.

21. Child-Safe Cleaning Supplies

- A small spray bottle with a mild cleaning solution for children to help clean up spills.

22. Light Switch Extender

- An extender or motion-activated light to allow the child to turn lights on and off independently.

The Entryway

Child-Sized Furniture and Fixtures

1. Low Hooks

- Install hooks at the child's height for coats, hats, and bags.

2. Shoe Rack or Tray

- A low shoe rack or a designated mat for organizing shoes.

3. Bench or Seat

- A small bench or chair where the child can sit while putting on or taking off shoes.

4. Mirror at Child's Height

- A shatterproof mirror for checking their appearance before leaving the house.

Organization and Storage

5. Cubbies or Baskets

- Use labeled or color-coded bins for items like gloves, scarves, and seasonal accessories.

6. Umbrella Stand

- A small, lightweight stand for the child to store their umbrella.

7. Bag Station

- A specific spot for backpacks, lunch bags, or daycare items.

8. Key Hook or Tray

- A low hook or small tray for older children to hang or place keys or small belongings.

Seasonal and Weather Essentials

9. Weather Gear

- Keep items like raincoats, boots, and hats accessible during relevant seasons.

10. Weather Chart or Checklist

- A small chart or picture guide to help the child prepare for the day's weather (e.g., "Do I need a jacket or a hat?").

11. Sunscreen or Bug Spray Station

- For older children, place these items in a safe spot for easy access.

Visual Reminders and Independence Tools

15. In and out Reminders

- A visual guide to help children remember what to take when leaving and where to store items when returning.

16. Name Labels or Photos

- Add labels or pictures to storage areas for non-readers to identify their belongings.

17. Clock or Timer

- A child-friendly clock or sand timer to help the child manage time while getting ready.

Safety and Comfort

18. Non-Slip Rug or Mat

- A sturdy mat for wiping feet and preventing slips.

19. Lighting

- Use soft, motion-activated lights to ensure the area is always well-lit for children.

20. Emergency Contact Information

- A small laminated card or list of emergency contacts and addresses, displayed at a child-friendly height.

Personal Touches

21. Family Photo or Art

- Hang a small family photo or artwork the child has created to personalize the space.

22. Nature Elements

- Include a small plant or seasonal items like pinecones to make the entryway warm and inviting.

23. Welcome Sign or Board

- A board where the child can draw or write messages to welcome visitors.

Visuals and Diagrams

Incorporating visual aids into your child's learning environment can significantly enhance their understanding and retention. Think of how a simple chart can transform a routine into a predictable, manageable part of the day. Daily routine charts, for instance, provide visual cues that help children anticipate what comes next, creating a sense of security and structure. These charts don't have to be elaborate; even a series of pictures representing different activities can guide your child through their day. Similarly, visual schedules for task management allow children to see tasks broken down into manageable steps, fostering independence and responsibility. When children can track their progress visually, they gain a sense of accomplishment that boosts confidence and motivation.

Creating effective educational diagrams doesn't require artistic prowess, just thoughtful design. Use color coding to organize information, making it easier for your child to process and understand. For example, different colors can represent various parts of their day or different categories of their tasks, like chores, homework, or playtime. Incorporating child-friendly illustrations adds an element of fun and engagement. Simple drawings or stickers can capture a child's attention, turning learning into an enjoyable activity. These visuals don't just make information accessible—they also encourage children to interact with it. As they engage with these diagrams, they develop skills in organizing and categorizing.

Incorporating visuals into your home environment blends learning with everyday activities. Labeling drawers and shelves with pictures or words allows your child to learn vocabulary and organization skills while keeping their space tidy. This practice teaches them where items belong, reducing clutter and fostering a sense of responsibility and order. Displaying artwork and educational posters invites learning into your living space. Choose images that inspire curiosity—maps, alphabets, or art prints. Rotate these visuals regularly to maintain interest and introduce new ideas.

Encouraging children to create their own visuals is a powerful way to reinforce their learning. Let them make personal storyboards that depict their favorite stories or daily routines. This activity boosts creativity and enhances comprehension as they translate ideas into images. Drawing maps of familiar places, like the route to school or the layout of your home, develops spatial awareness and memory. These projects invite children to take ownership of their learning process, building confidence in their abilities. As they express their ideas visually, they learn to communicate complex thoughts in simple, understandable ways.

By integrating these visual elements into your home, you create an environment where learning naturally weaves into the fabric of daily life. Visual aids serve as bridges between abstract concepts and tangible understanding, making learning accessible and enjoyable.

Next, we'll explore how these foundations of order and creativity extend into the day-to-day routines, empowering your child to take charge of their self-care and education.

CHAPTER 6
DAILY ROUTINES THE MONTESSORI WAY

In the whirlwind of daily life, establishing a Montessori-inspired routine can bring a sense of calm and order. What we want is to strike the right balance between structure and freedom. Think of the day as a gentle ebb and flow, where structured moments provide security, and free play offers freedom. Start with a morning routine that includes time for personal care, a healthy breakfast, and perhaps a moment of mindfulness or reflection. This sets a positive tone for the day, giving children the structure they crave while allowing room for spontaneity. As the day progresses, alternate between guided learning activities and periods of unstructured play. This variety keeps children engaged and excited, allowing them to explore their interests while still benefiting from the guidance of structured tasks. Let your schedule be flexible; allowing for natural transitions between activities helps children adjust smoothly, reducing stress and fostering adaptability.

Incorporating practical life activities into your daily routine is at the core of the Montessori method. It seamlessly blends learning with everyday tasks, transforming mundane chores into valuable lessons and enjoyable moments. Consider involving your child in setting the table during meal preparation. This simple task teaches them about organization, responsibility, and the importance of contributing to the family. After play sessions, involve them in tidying up. Encourage them to sort toys, put away art supplies, and ensure everything is in its place. These tasks instill a sense of ownership and responsibility, teaching children that maintaining their environment is an integral part of daily life.

Promoting rhythm and consistency in daily routines offers numerous benefits for children. A predictable routine provides a sense of security, allowing children to anticipate what's coming next and prepare themselves mentally and emotionally. Morning rituals are a great way to start the day, whether it's a simple checklist of activities or a family breakfast where everyone gathers to discuss the day's plans. In the evening, wind-down activities like reading a book, listening to calming music, or engaging in a quiet craft can help children transition from the excitement of the day to the peace of bedtime. These rituals create a comforting rhythm, supporting emotional well-being and reinforcing the values of routine and reliability.

Adapting routines to fit the unique needs of your family is crucial. No two families are alike, and what works for one may not suit another. Tailor activities based on your family's dynamics, considering factors like work schedules, extracurricular commitments, and individual preferences. Flexibility is key—allow for adjustments and changes as needed. Perhaps your child prefers an earlier bedtime, or maybe they thrive with a bit more free play in the afternoon. Be open to experimentation, adjusting the routine to find what best supports your child's development and your family's harmony. This adaptability ensures that the routine remains a source of support rather than stress, encouraging growth and connection within the family unit.

In this section, we will first look at examples of different routines of the day for a child growing in a Montessori home. The activities and tasks' difficulty level will vary widely, between 6 months and 5 years of age. The aim of this section is not to give you perfect routine examples for every age group, but to give a general yet detailed idea of daily routines that you can adapt to your child's age and ability level. Notice how everything the child does ties to the prepared environment we have carefully designed in the previous chapter. Also, notice how the child flows easily from one task to the next when everything is accessible and in order. Note that I have highlighted the most important keywords, to give you an idea of what to include when creating your own routine chart with your child. We will then take a look at simple examples of routine charts that will help crystallize the idea of a structure in which the child can blossom into an independent and confident little human.

Examples of Montessori-Infused Daily Routines

Morning Routine

- The child wakes up and gets off their floor bed by themselves.
- Makes their **bed** to the best of their ability.
- Goes to the bathroom, where the potty or the child-adapted **toilet** seat is easily accessible.
- Climbs the stool to access the sink, where they **wash** their **hands** using mild soap.
- Takes a washcloth from the nearby basket on the counter and **wash**es their **face**.
- Dries their hands and face on a clean towel.
- Takes their toothbrush and toothpaste from the cup sitting near the sink and **brush**es their **teeth**.
- Rinses their mouth with an empty cup sitting near the sink.
- Goes back to their room where they select their clothes for the day.
- Takes clothes from the drawers, bins, or rack, and **dress** themselves in front of the mirror.
- Takes the hairbrush from the drawer and **brush**es their **hair**.

Daily Routines the Montessori way | 103

Morning Routine Chart Example

Make bed

toilet

wash hands

Brush teeth

Dress

Hair

Mealtime Routine

- The child **wash**es their **hands** in the kitchen sink with the help of a stool. Dries their hands on the hand towel.

- Takes a small wash cloth from a bin or drawer and pours a small amount of water on it from the sink.

- Puts the wash cloth on the table.

- **Set**s the **table**. Takes utensils from the drawer and places them on the table, occasionally referring to the visual aid for the correct utensils' placement.

- Does the same with dishes and cups.

- Pours water in a small cup using the water dispenser or a small pitcher, and puts their cup on the table.

- Puts their bib or **apron** on.

- Sits down and spreads avocado purée on toast with a small butter knife.

- **Eat**s and drinks.

- **Wash**es their **hands and face** with the wet wash cloth.

- Takes their **dish** and cup and puts them **in**to the kitchen **sink**.

- Picks up the small broom and dustpan and **clean**s **up** the small crumbs of toast that accidentally fell on the floor while eating.

- Empties the dustpan into the garbage bin and puts the broom and dustpan away.

Evening Routine

- The child is offered several choices of **wind-down activities** such as reading, puzzles, or drawing.
- Undresses for **bath** time and chooses a toy or helps pouring bubble soap in the water.
- **Wash**es themselves.
- Takes a clean towel and dries themselves.
- Chooses their **pajamas** and put them on.
- Takes the hairbrush out of the drawer and **brush**es their **hair**.
- Reaches for their toothbrush and toothpaste and **brush**es their **teeth**.
- Rinses their mouth with the nearby cup.
- **Tidi**es **up** by putting away any remaining toys, books, or materials.
- Chooses one or two books for **bedtime stories**.
- Shares a moment of **gratitude** with the parent by talking about something they enjoyed during the day, and what they are excited about for tomorrow.
- Listens to the parent singing a lullaby or use positive affirmations such as ''We love you very much.'' ''You are doing great.'' ''We are proud of you.''
- Kisses and hugs.
- **Sleep**s.

Evening Routine Chart Example

toilet	bath	brush hair	brush teeth	pajamas	bedtime story	sleep

Tips to Increase the Success of Daily Routines

1. Establish Predictable Routines

Consistency is Key:

Keep routines consistent each day to help the child internalize the sequence of tasks and build a sense of security.

Use Visual Schedules:

Create a routine chart with pictures and simple words to give children a clear understanding of what comes next.

2. Provide Clear Cues

Verbal Cues:

Give calm and positive reminders, such as, "In 5 minutes, it will be time to tidy up your toys."

Non-Verbal Cues:

Use visual or auditory signals, like turning off a light or ringing a small bell, to indicate transitions between activities.

Timers:

Use a sand timer or a simple digital timer to help children manage time and understand when tasks should begin or end.

3. Prepare the Environment

Keep It Tidy and Organized:

Maintain a clutter-free environment where everything has a designated place to promote order and reduce distractions.

Dim the lights during the evening

Gradually reduce lighting to signal that bedtime is approaching and support the body's natural sleep cues.

Make Tools Accessible

Provide the child with everything they need to complete the tasks at hand.

Simplify Choices

Limit the number of items available (2-3 outfits or toys) to make decision-making easier and reduce overwhelm.

4. Foster Independence

Encourage Self-Initiated Actions

Allow children to attempt tasks like dressing, cleaning, or preparing their own snacks, even if it takes longer.

Teach Skills Gradually

Break tasks into manageable steps and model them slowly for the child to observe and imitate.

Provide Time for Practice

Allow extra time for the child to complete tasks independently without feeling rushed.

5. Use Positive Reinforcement

Celebrate Efforts, Not Just Results

Praise the child's effort with specific feedback, like, "Congratulations for not giving up easily!"

Offer Encouragement

Use empowering phrases like, "Wow you are getting good at this!" to motivate the child to keep practicing.

6. Anticipate and Prevent Challenges

Plan Ahead

Prepare materials, clothes, or meals in advance to minimize delays and potential frustration.

Provide Transition Time

Give the child ample warning before moving to the next activity to avoid abrupt interruptions.

Minimize Distractions

Turn off unnecessary screens or background noise to help the child focus on the current task.

7. Encourage Responsibility

Involve the Child in Tasks

Let the child take part in tidying up, setting the table, or organizing their belongings to foster ownership and accountability.

Create Logical Consequences

For example, if toys are not put away, they might not be available until the child helps tidy up.

8. Maintain a Calm and Patient Demeanor

Stay Calm During Setbacks

Avoid showing frustration when routines don't go perfectly; instead, guide the child gently back on track.

Model the Desired Behavior

Demonstrate actions like tidying up or brushing teeth to inspire imitation.

9. Adjust as Needed

Observe and Adapt

Watch for signs of fatigue, boredom, or frustration, and adjust the routine or tasks accordingly.

Simplify Overwhelming Tasks

If a task is too complex, break it down into smaller, more manageable steps for the child.

10. End on a Positive Note

Reflect on Successes

At the end of the day, discuss what went well and acknowledge the child's contributions to the routine.

Celebrate Completion

Use a small ritual, like a high-five or a shared song, to mark the successful completion of the routine.

Balancing Montessori with Other Parenting Styles

After reading this book, you may be wondering if you need to drop everything you hear from other parenting philosophies and concentrate only on Montessori. Here's the good news: you don't have to stick to a single doctrine. Harmonizing Montessori with other parenting styles is not only possible but can be incredibly rewarding. The first step is identifying your core values and goals as a parent. What principles do you hold dear? Is it fostering independence, encouraging creativity, or perhaps promoting empathy? By understanding these priorities, you can weave Montessori principles into your existing parenting framework. Finding common ground between different methods allows you to create a unique parenting style that resonates with your family's needs and aspirations, offering a balanced approach that feels authentic and effective.

Customizing Montessori principles to fit your family's lifestyle is about flexibility and creativity. You might choose to mix traditional toys with Montessori materials, embracing the diversity of educational tools available. For example, incorporating blocks and puzzles alongside Montessori-style trays and baskets provides a rich environment for exploration and learning. Balancing structured activities with free play is another way to adapt Montessori to your unique home dynamics. While Montessori emphasizes self-directed learning, you can still integrate structured activities that align with other educational philosophies you value. Perhaps you schedule specific times for guided learning, like music or art lessons, while leaving ample space for your child to explore freely. This blend not only honors Montessori's core principles but also caters to your child's diverse interests and developmental needs.

Consistency is key when involving all caregivers in your child's upbringing. Whether it's grandparents, nannies, or babysitters, everyone should be on the same page regarding your parenting approach. Share Montessori techniques with family members, explaining the reasoning behind the practices. This might include demonstrating how to set up a Montessori-inspired activity, or discussing the importance of observation and minimal intervention. Holding regular discussions on parenting approaches ensures that everyone understands and respects your chosen methods. These conversations create a supportive network where caregivers feel empowered to contribute to your child's development in meaningful ways. By fostering this sense of unity, you create a stable and nurturing environment for your child.

Crafting a Personalized Montessori Action Plan

Creating a personalized Montessori action plan begins with understanding your family's unique dynamics, which can significantly impact your approach to education and parenting. It's important to identify specific developmental goals for each child, considering their interests, strengths, and areas for improvement. As you reflect on these elements, think about what you hope to achieve in the short and long term. Whether it's fostering independence, enhancing language skills, or developing social competencies, having clear objectives will guide your efforts and provide a framework for growth. Prioritizing these goals helps you allocate time and resources effectively, ensuring that you focus on what truly matters for your child's development.

Once you've established your goals, designing a flexible action plan becomes the next step. A well-crafted plan should include both short-term and long-term objectives, allowing you to track progress and adjust as needed. Short-term goals might involve introducing new activities or setting up a Montessori-inspired space, while long-term goals could focus on fostering specific skills over time. Flexibility is key, as children's needs and interests evolve, and your plan should be adaptable to accommodate these changes. Regularly incorporating feedback and adjustments ensures that your approach remains relevant and effective. This dynamic process not only keeps you engaged but also reinforces your commitment to nurturing your child's potential.

Implementing and evaluating your plan involves putting your strategies into action and monitoring their effectiveness. Regularly reviewing and revising the plan allows you to assess what's working and what might need tweaking. Celebrate achievements and milestones, no matter how small, to recognize your child's progress and to motivate continued growth. This positive reinforcement builds confidence and encourages a love for learning. As you evaluate progress, consider how each step aligns with your family's overarching goals and values. This reflection not only keeps you on track but also deepens your understanding of your child's development, fostering a more intentional and informed approach to parenting.

Building a supportive network is an invaluable aspect of your Montessori journey. Connecting with other Montessori families, whether locally or online, provides a wealth of resources, advice, and camaraderie. These communities offer opportunities to share experiences, discuss challenges, and celebrate successes. They can also be a source of inspiration, introducing new ideas and activities that you might not have considered. Engaging with a network of like-minded parents fosters a sense of belonging and support, helping you stay motivated and informed. This collaborative spirit not only enriches your approach but also creates a nurturing environment for your child, grounded in shared values and goals.

In crafting your personalized Montessori action plan, you're setting the stage for a thoughtful, intentional approach to parenting and education. By understanding your family's needs, designing a flexible plan, implementing strategies, and building a supportive network, you're creating a foundation that supports your child's growth and development. This holistic approach aligns with Montessori principles and also resonates with your family's unique dynamics and aspirations. As you navigate this process, remember that it's a journey of discovery and growth, both for you and your child. Realize that you and your child will never reach perfection because it is already perfect just as it is! Embrace the fact that growth never ends, and that the secret lies in enjoying each step of the way as much as you can.

CONCLUSION

As we wrap up this exploration of the Montessori approach, let's take a moment to revisit the heart of what we've explored together. At the core of the Montessori philosophy are four guiding principles: respect for the child, the absorbent mind, self-directed learning, and holistic development. Each principle shapes how we view and interact with our children, emphasizing their unique capabilities and innate desire to learn. By respecting the child, we acknowledge their individuality and potential. The absorbent mind reminds us of a child's incredible capacity to soak up knowledge from their environment. Self-directed learning encourages us to trust in their natural curiosity, while holistic development ensures we're nurturing every aspect of their growth.

Practical application is where the magic happens. We've discussed how to weave Montessori principles into your home, room by room. From designing child-friendly spaces to incorporating daily routines, you've got a toolkit brimming with ideas. Consider starting small—perhaps a low shelf in the living room for toys or a simple routine for morning self-directed play. Consider making a list of the things you would like to incorporate in your life, and take on one item at a time. These manageable steps lay the groundwork for a Montessori-inspired environment. Remember, it's about creating spaces that invite exploration and independence. As you make these changes, observe how your child interacts with their surroundings and adapt accordingly. This ongoing process of adjustment and reflection is essential.

Now, here's where the real adventure begins. I invite you to take what you've learned and put it into practice. Start with what resonates most, and build from there. Montessori is flexible and adaptable. It's about finding what works for your family. Trust in your ability to create a nurturing environment that supports your child's growth. Embrace the trial and error, and know that each effort you make is a step towards enriching your child's life.

Confidence in your parenting is key. You've got the resources, and more importantly, the heart to make it happen. Trust yourself and your instincts. Remember, you're not alone. There are communities of parents, educators, and resources ready to support you. Dive into Montessori groups online or in your local area. Share experiences, ask questions, and learn from others. The Montessori community is a treasure trove of wisdom and support, waiting to welcome you.

Finally, a personal note from me to you: Thank you for allowing me to accompany you on this journey. Your dedication to nurturing your child's development is what gives purpose to my work. I hope this book has been a helpful guide, offering clarity and encouragement along the way. As you continue to explore and implement Montessori principles, know that you're making a difference in your child's life and in the world they will one day inherit and shape.

Keep nurturing, keep exploring, and keep believing in the incredible potential within each child. The world of

Montessori is vast and full of possibilities—I'm excited to know where it can take you and your family. Thank you for being a part of this change, and for allowing the Montessori method to inspire and enrich your home. Here's to endless learning and boundless curiosity!

With love,

Kim Suzuki

Did you like the book?

Did you find the book useful? Were you inspired by one section more than the others? Are you excited about implementing the Montessori Method into your home? Whatever it is, I'd love to hear it! Please consider leaving a review or a simple star-rating on Amazon. By doing so, you are supporting me tremendously, as well as countless parents looking for valuable information on parenting.

Thank you!!!

Kim Suzuki

ACTIVITIES LIST

Notes On The Activities List

- This list is separated by age group in five main sections: 0 to 12 months, 12 to 24 months, 2 to 3, 3 to 4, and 4 to 5.

- Each main section is organized by activity type, such as *Arts and Crafts*, *Sensory and Motor Skills*, *Social and Emotional Development*, etc.

- Each activity in the list contains a brief description of the activity, a list of benefits, and suggested variations to keep the activity interesting for the child.

- The list is image-free as to include a maximum number of activities in the book. If a particular activity idea is not clear to you due to the absence of visual support, we invite you to look it up on the internet to get more information and images related to it.

- Some toys are sometimes mentioned, but not described in detail. (Example: Montessori Sound Cylinders) If you are not familiar with a particular object that is referred to, again we invite you to look it up on the internet, as there are plenty of images, videos, and text descriptions on these particular toys.

- Some activities will show up in more than one age group. Remember that although we kept the development stage of the child in mind when organizing this activities list, each child's development is different. You are invited to try activities that are not in the corresponding age group of your child if you feel like a certain activity would be fun and appropriate.

- Have fun! Some activities will work right away, and some won't. But the way in which the activity is presented to the child and your personal enthusiasm about it will have a major influence on how the child adopts it. Be creative and flexible and do your best to adapt the activities to your child's unique situation.

0-12 MONTHS

Sensory Exploration Activities

Sensory Treasure Basket

Description: Fill a basket with various textured objects (fabrics, soft toys, wooden items) for your baby to touch, explore, and grasp.

Benefits: Stimulates sensory development, encourages fine motor skills, and fosters curiosity.

Variations: Rotate the items regularly to maintain interest.

High-Contrast Black and White Cards

Description: Show your baby black and white pattern cards to enhance visual development.

Benefits: Enhances visual tracking and focus.

Variations: Introduce colorful cards as your baby grows.

Mirror Exploration

Description: Show your baby their reflection in a baby-safe mirror.

Benefits: Boosts self-awareness and visual tracking skills.

Variations: Use different types of mirrors, such as curved or fun-shaped ones.

Soft Fabric Scrap Play

Description: Provide an assortment of soft fabric scraps for your baby to touch, squeeze, and explore.

Benefits: Stimulates tactile exploration and sensory development.

Variations: Offer different types of fabric, such as silk, cotton, and fleece.

Nature Mobile

Description: Create a mobile with natural objects like pinecones, leaves, and feathers for your baby to observe and touch.

Benefits: Enhances visual tracking, nature appreciation, and sensory exploration.

Variations: Change the mobile components with the seasons.

Fruit and Vegetable Exploration

Description: Offer age-appropriate fruits and vegetables for your baby to touch, taste, and explore.

Benefits: Introduces new textures, flavors, and sensory experiences.

Variations: Explore a variety of fruits and vegetables.

Texture Sensory Bags

Description: Fill sealable plastic bags with various textures (rice, fabric, gel, water) for your baby to touch and squish.

Benefits: Encourages tactile exploration and sensory stimulation.

Variations: You can add colorful objects or foods, such as beads or sprinkles.

Texture Boards

Description: Create boards with various textured materials (sandpaper, fabric, velvet) for your baby to touch.

Benefits: Enhances tactile exploration and sensory development.

Variations: Use different textures and materials.

Texture Wall Art

Description: Hang textured art pieces at your baby's eye level for them to reach out and feel.

Benefits: Encourages sensory exploration and art appreciation.

Variations: Use different textured materials in the artwork.

Texture Walk

Description: Create a soft texture walkway using materials like fleece, sandpaper, or bubble wrap for your baby to explore while crawling.

Benefits: Enhances tactile and sensory awareness during movement.

Variations: Change the textures periodically.

Texture Books

Description: Create fabric or sensory texture books for your baby to explore through touch.

Benefits: Encourages sensory exploration and tactile discrimination.

Variations: Include different textures and materials in the books.

Motor Skill Development Activities

Sensory Board

Description: Create a sensory board with various textures and objects (e.g., buttons, key chains, zippers, ribbons, switches, locks, gears, etc.) for your baby to touch and manipulate.

Benefits: Enhances fine motor skills and sensory exploration.

Variations: Add or change textures and objects based on your baby's interests.

Tummy Time Play

Description: Place your baby on their tummy on a soft mat to encourage neck and upper body strength.

Benefits: Supports physical development and helps prevent flat head syndrome.

Variations: Add a mirror, toys, or interesting objects to engage your baby.

Baby Gym

Description: Set up a simple baby gym with hanging toys for your baby to reach.

Benefits: Enhances gross motor skills and hand-eye coordination.

Variations: Change the hanging toys to keep it interesting.

Soft Ball Rolling

Description: Roll a soft, lightweight ball towards your baby to encourage reaching and grasping.

Benefits: Develops hand-eye coordination and strengthens arm muscles.

Variations: Use balls of different sizes and textures.

Rattle Play

Description: Offer rattles with different sounds and textures for your baby to shake and explore.

Benefits: Enhances auditory and tactile sensory development.

Variations: Rotate the rattles to introduce new sounds.

Foot Painting

Description: Dip your baby's feet in baby-safe paint and let them make footprints on paper.

Benefits: Encourages foot and leg movement and introduces early art exploration.

Variations: Use different colors of washable, non-toxic paint.

Obstacle Course

Description: Create a safe, low obstacle course with pillows and soft objects for your baby to crawl or roll over.

Benefits: Enhances gross motor skills and spatial awareness.

Variations: Change the course layout periodically.

Baby Yoga

Description: Engage in gentle baby yoga poses and stretches with your baby, helping them move and stretch their limbs.

Benefits: Supports physical development, flexibility, and bonding.

Variations: Explore different baby yoga poses.

Cognitive Development Activities

High-Contrast Mobile

Description: Hang a black and white mobile above the crib to engage your baby's visual focus.

Benefits: Enhances visual tracking and concentration.

Variations: Introduce other visually stimulating mobiles.

Peek-a-Boo

Description: Play peek-a-boo with a soft cloth or blanket to teach object permanence.

Benefits: Enhances cognitive development and understanding of object permanence.

Variations: Try peek-a-boo with different objects.

Exploring Household Items

Description: Allow your baby to safely explore everyday objects like wooden spoons, cups, or scarves.

Benefits: Encourages curiosity, and object manipulation.

Variations: Introduce new household items for exploration.

Object Permanence Box

Description: Introduce an object permanence box with a small ball for your baby to practice dropping and retrieving.

Benefits: Develops the understanding of object permanence and fine motor skills.

Variations: Try boxes with different openings.

Early Math with Counting Toys

Description: Offer counting toys like stacking rings or nesting cups for your baby to explore and practice basic counting skills.

Benefits: Introduces early math concepts and fine motor development.

Variations: Explore toys with different shapes and numbers.

Object Exploration Tray

Description: Create a tray with various objects for your baby to examine, touch, and manipulate.

Benefits: Encourages curiosity, problem-solving, and exploration.

Variations: Rotate the objects regularly.

Shadow Play

Description: Use a flashlight to create simple shadow shapes on the wall for your baby to watch and explore.

Benefits: Enhances visual tracking, observation skills, and imagination.

Variations: Experiment with different shadow shapes.

Language Development Activities

Reading Aloud

Description: Read age-appropriate books to your baby, describing the pictures and engaging in conversation.

Benefits: Promotes language development, vocabulary, and bonding.

Variations: Explore different books and topics.

Singing Songs and Nursery Rhymes

Description: Sing lullabies and nursery rhymes to your baby, incorporating hand movements or actions.

Benefits: Encourages language development, rhythm, and social interaction.

Variations: Introduce new songs and actions.

Sound Imitation

Description: Make simple sounds like clapping, blowing kisses, or animal sounds and encourage your baby to imitate.

Benefits: Enhances sound recognition and early communication skills.

Variations: Introduce new sounds and actions.

Baby Sign Language

Description: Begin teaching simple baby sign language gestures like "more," "eat," ''milk'', or "all done."

Benefits: Facilitates early communication and reduces frustration.

Variations: Add more signs as your baby progresses.

Story Baskets

Description: Create story baskets with toys or objects related to a specific story and engage in storytelling with your baby.

Benefits: Promotes language comprehension, imagination, and storytelling skills.

Variations: Explore different story themes and objects.

Baby Babble Conversations

Description: Engage in "conversations" with your baby by responding to their coos, babbling, and vocalizations.

Benefits: Promotes early communication skills and bonding.

Variations: Mimic your baby's sounds and respond with enthusiasm.

Interactive Storytelling

Description: Tell interactive stories using simple props or puppets to engage your baby's attention and imagination.

Benefits: Enhances language development, creativity, and storytelling skills.

Variations: Create different story themes.

Social, Bonding, and Emotional Development Activities

Emotion Mirroring

Description: Mirror your baby's facial expressions and emotions to help them understand and express their feelings.

Benefits: Supports emotional development and empathy.

Variations: Try different facial expressions and emotions.

Family Photo Conversation

Description: Arrange photos of family members in front of your baby and describe each person, fostering a sense of family connection.

Benefits: Promotes language development, family recognition, and bonding.

Variations: Share stories or memories about each family member.

Social Interaction

Description: Encourage interactions with family members and peers through playdates and gentle social exposure.

Benefits: Develops social skills, communication, and emotional regulation.

Variations: Arrange playdates with different children.

Baby-Wearing

Description: Use a baby carrier or sling to keep your baby close while you go about your daily activities.

Benefits: Provides physical closeness, comfort, and security for your baby.

Variations: Explore different types of baby carriers.

Baby Massage

Description: Gently massage your baby using baby-safe oil, following gentle and soothing strokes.

Benefits: Promotes relaxation, enhances bonding, and stimulates sensory awareness.

Variations: Explore different massage techniques and rhythms.

Reading Together

Description: Choose age-appropriate books and read to your baby, making eye contact and using varying tones and expressions.

Benefits: Enhances language development, comprehension, and bonding.

Variations: Offer different books and themes.

Soft Toy Friends

Description: Provide soft and cuddly toys for your baby to interact with, cuddle, and bond with.

Benefits: Encourages attachment, emotional comfort, and sensory exploration.

Variations: Rotate soft toys to keep them interesting.

Calm and Quiet Time

Description: Create a calm and quiet environment for you and your baby, dimming lights, playing soft music, or using white noise.. Meditate or relax while your baby is present and observes you.

Benefits: Encourages relaxation, sensory awareness, and better sleep.

Variations: Experiment with different calming techniques.

Emotion Exploration

Description: Show pictures or drawings of different facial expressions to your baby and describe the associated emotions.

Benefits: Helps your baby recognize emotions and fosters empathy.

Variations: Use photos of family members displaying emotions.

Tickle Play

Description: Engage in gentle tickle play with your baby, using soft touches and playful sounds.

Benefits: Promotes bonding, laughter, and sensory awareness.

Variations: Tickle different parts of the body.

Mirror Dance

Description: Hold your baby in front of a full-length mirror and sway or dance together while making eye contact.

Benefits: Enhances body awareness, coordination, and bonding.

Variations: Play calming music during mirror time.

Practical Life Activities

Baby-Safe Cleaning Supplies

Description: Allow your baby to explore baby-safe cleaning supplies like a small broom or a cloth for gentle cleaning play.

Benefits: Fosters a sense of responsibility and involvement in daily tasks.

Variations: Clean different objects around the house.

Mealtime Observation

Description: Allow your baby to observe meal preparation and join you at the table during mealtime.

Benefits: Fosters a sense of inclusion, family bonding, and early exposure to food.

Variations: Offer baby-safe utensils to explore.

Laundry Basket Exploration

Description: Place your baby in a clean, empty laundry basket for them to sit in and explore.

Benefits: Encourages spatial awareness and offers a change of perspective.

Variations: Add soft toys or fabrics for sensory exploration, and change the location and height of the basket.

Stacking Cups

Description: Provide stacking cups for your baby to practice nesting and stacking.

Benefits: Enhances fine motor skills, coordination, and problem-solving.

Variations: Use cups of different sizes and materials. During bath time once your baby can sit by themselves..

Dressing Routine

Description: Involve your baby in the dressing routine by allowing them to hold items or put their arms through sleeves.

Benefits: Promotes independence and familiarity with daily routines.

Variations: Use clothing with large, easy-to-manipulate buttons or snaps.

Sock Matching

Description: Offer a pile of baby socks for your baby to practice matching by pairs.

Benefits: Introduces basic sorting skills and hand-eye coordination.

Variations: Use socks with different colors or patterns.

Feeding Independence

Description: Encourage self-feeding by providing age-appropriate finger foods and a safe feeding environment.

Benefits: Promotes independence, fine motor skills, and a positive relationship with food.

Variations: Offer a variety of healthy finger foods.

Gentle Toothbrush Play

Description: Offer a soft baby toothbrush for your baby to explore by touching their gums or practicing brushing.

Benefits: Introduces oral hygiene awareness and sensory exploration.

Variations: Use a baby-friendly toothpaste if desired.

Outdoor and Nature Activities

Nature Walks

Description: Take your baby on gentle nature walks to explore the outdoors and observe natural surroundings.

Benefits: Stimulates sensory exploration, connection with nature, and fresh air exposure.

Variations: Visit different natural settings.

Gentle Playground Exploration

Description: Visit baby-friendly playgrounds with simple equipment for exploration.

Benefits: Supports gross motor development and social exposure.

Variations: Choose playgrounds suitable for young babies.

Leaf and Flower Sensory Exploration

Description: Collect leaves and flowers during nature walks and let your baby touch, smell and explore them.

Benefits: Enhances sensory exploration, nature appreciation, and outdoor bonding.

Variations: Discover different types of leaves and flowers, in different settings such as forests, gardens, parks, etc.

Outdoor Picnics

Description: Enjoy outdoor picnics with age-appropriate finger foods, encouraging sensory exploration and outdoor dining.

Benefits: Fosters a love for nature, family bonding, and sensory experiences.

Variations: Picnic in various outdoor settings.

Gentle Water Splashing

Description: Fill a shallow container with a small amount of water for your baby to explore by splashing gently.

Benefits: Introduces water sensory experiences and hand-eye coordination.

Variations: Use different containers and outdoor settings.

Sand Play

Description: Provide a baby-friendly sandpit for your baby to touch and explore sand using safe sand toys.

Benefits: Stimulates tactile exploration, creativity, and outdoor play.

Variations: Add water to the sand to enhance tactile exploration.

Music and Sound Activities

Musical Shakers

Description: Fill small bottles with various materials (rice, beans, bells) for your baby to shake and hear different sounds.

Benefits: Enhances auditory exploration and sound discrimination. Encourages rhythm and coordination.

Variations: Experiment with different fillings and container sizes for varied sounds.

Musical Sing-Along

Description: Sing simple songs to your baby and use instruments like a small xylophone or handbells for added musical exploration.

Benefits: Enhances auditory perception, language development, and appreciation for music.

Variations: Explore various songs and instruments.

Instrument Exploration

Description: Provide a variety of musical instruments for your baby to touch, explore, and create sounds.

Benefits: Enhances auditory exploration, rhythm, and creativity.

Variations: Offer a wide range of instruments to experiment with.

Storytelling with Sound Effects

Description: Tell stories to your baby using sound effects or simple musical instruments to create an interactive narrative.

Benefits: Stimulates imagination, language development, and engagement.

Variations: Create unique stories with different themes.

Gentle Lullabies

Description: Sing lullabies to your baby at naptime and bedtime to establish a calming bedtime routine.

Benefits: Encourages relaxation, sleep routine development, and bonding.

Variations: Choose soothing lullabies and melodies.

Rhyme and Rhythm Books

Description: Read rhythmic and rhyming books to your baby, emphasizing the cadence and rhythm of the words.

Benefits: Enhances language development, rhythm perception, and phonemic awareness.

Variations: Explore different rhyming books.

Nature's Symphony

Description: Put yourself and your baby in an environment rich with sounds, without any distractions such as toys, and listen to the sounds of nature like wind rustling through trees, waves crashing, or rain falling.

Benefits: Encourages auditory exploration, relaxation, and appreciation for the natural world.

Variations: Explore different natural soundscapes.

12-24 MONTHS

Fine Motor Skill Development Activities

Stacking Cups

Description: Provide a set of stacking cups for your toddler to stack, nest, and explore.

Benefits: Enhances fine motor skills, hand-eye coordination, and spatial awareness.

Variations: Experiment with cups of different sizes and materials.

Pegging Activities

Description: Offer a pegboard with large pegs for your toddler to insert and remove, developing fine motor control and hand strength.

Benefits: Promotes hand-eye coordination, problem-solving, and patience.

Variations: Use pegs of various shapes and colors.

Lacing and Threading

Description: Provide lacing cards and strings or shoelaces for your toddler to practice threading.

Benefits: Develops fine motor skills, hand-eye coordination, and concentration.

Variations: Explore different lacing card designs.

Pouring and Transferring

Description: Offer small containers and objects for your toddler to practice pouring and transferring items between containers.

Benefits: Enhances fine motor control, hand strength, and concentration.

Variations: Use different objects and container sizes.

Buttoning and Snapping

Description: Introduce clothing items with buttons or snaps, allowing your toddler to practice fastening and unfastening.

Benefits: Develops fine motor skills, finger dexterity, and dressing independence.

Variations: Use clothes with different fasteners.

Clay Sculpting

Description: Provide child-safe clay or playdough and encourage the child to sculpt objects or shapes.

Benefits: Develops fine motor skills, creativity, and a sense of 3D form.

Variations: Use different types of clay or introduce tools for sculpting.

Sensory Exploration Activities

Sensory Bin Exploration

Description: Fill a shallow container with materials like rice, sand, or beans for tactile exploration.

Benefits: Enhances sensory awareness, fine motor skills, and imaginative play.

Variations: Change the materials for new textures and experiences.

Nature Scavenger Hunt

Description: Create a list of natural items with images for your toddler to find during outdoor walks, promoting observation skills and a love for nature.

Benefits: Encourages outdoor exploration, connection with nature, and vocabulary development.

Variations: Adjust the list based on the season or location.

Finger Painting

Description: Allow your toddler to finger paint with non-toxic, washable paint on large paper.

Benefits: Promotes creativity, fine motor skills, and sensory exploration.

Variations: Use various colors and different painting tools or feet instead of hands.

Sensory Board

Description: Create a sensory board with various textures and objects (e.g., buttons, key chains, zippers, ribbons, switches, locks, gears, etc.) for your baby to touch and manipulate.

Benefits: Enhances fine motor skills and sensory exploration.

Variations: Add or change textures and objects based on your child's interests.

Nature's Sensory Bin

Description: Create a sensory bin with natural materials like sand, pinecones, and shells for tactile exploration.

Benefits: Stimulates sensory exploration, fine motor skills, and creativity.

Variations: Use different natural materials.

Practical Life Activities

Dressing Independence

Description: Encourage your toddler to dress themselves with simple clothing items like pants, shirts with large buttons, rain boots, hat, etc.

Benefits: Promotes independence, fine motor skills, and self-confidence.

Variations: Gradually introduce more complex clothing items.

Meal Preparation

Description: Involve your toddler in simple meal preparation tasks like washing vegetables, mixing, or spreading butter on bread,

Benefits: Fosters independence, fine motor skills, and an appreciation for cooking.

Variations: Try age-appropriate kitchen tasks.

Planting Seeds

Description: Plant seeds or seedlings with your toddler in a garden or indoor pot, allowing them to care for the plants.

Benefits: Nurtures a connection with nature, responsibility, and patience.

Variations: Choose different types of plants.

Feeding Pets

Description: Encourage your toddler to help feed and care for family pets, fostering a sense of responsibility and empathy.

Benefits: Teaches responsibility, empathy, and a love for animals.

Variations: Involve your toddler in pet grooming tasks.

Dressing and Undressing Dolls

Description: Provide dolls or stuffed animals with removable clothing and demonstrate how to dress and undress them.

Benefits: Encourages independence, fine motor skills, and self-help skills.

Variations: Use different dolls or introduce more complex clothing items.

Helping with Daily Chores

Description: Involve your child in simple daily chores like setting the table or putting away toys.

Benefits: Fosters a sense of contribution, responsibility, and cooperation.

Variations: Introduce new chores as your child grows.

Outdoor and Nature Activities

Water Painting

Description: Offer a water container with brushes of different sizes for your toddler to paint on a concrete wall.

Benefits: Stimulates creativity, hand-eye coordination, and relaxation.

Variations: Use colored water or different brushes.

Nature Art with Leaves

Description: Collect leaves during outdoor walks and use them to create art by gluing them onto paper.

Benefits: Enhances creativity, fine motor skills, and a connection with nature.

Variations: Create leaf rubbings or leaf collages.

Nature Scavenger Hunt

Description: Create a list of natural items (e.g., pinecones, acorns, feathers) for your toddler to find during outdoor adventures.

Benefits: Promotes observation skills, nature appreciation, and excitement for exploration.

Variations: Customize scavenger hunts for different outdoor locations.

Outdoor Picnics

Description: Enjoy outdoor picnics with toddler-friendly finger foods, encouraging outdoor dining and exploration.

Benefits: Fosters a love for nature, family bonding, and sensory experiences.

Variations: Change the picnic location.

Outdoor Obstacle Course

Description: Set up a safe, age-appropriate obstacle course with items like cones, hoops, and tunnels for your toddler to navigate.

Benefits: Enhances gross motor skills, coordination, and physical confidence.

Variations: Change the course layout regularly.

Bird Watching

Description: Set up bird feeders and binoculars for your toddler to observe and identify birds in your backyard or at a local park.

Benefits: Enhances observation skills, bird identification, and nature appreciation.

Variations: Learn about different bird species.

Nature Collections

Description: Go on nature walks with your toddler to collect and document interesting natural items like leaves, rocks, or shells.

Benefits: Fosters a connection with nature, observation skills, and an appreciation for the outdoors.

Variations: Create themed nature collections.

Gardening Together

Description: Involve your toddler in gardening tasks like planting, watering, and weeding in a garden or plant pots.

Benefits: Nurtures a love for gardening, responsibility, and sensory exploration.

Variations: Choose different plants or vegetables to grow.

Rock Painting

Description: Gather smooth rocks and paint them with your toddler, encouraging creativity and nature-themed designs.

Benefits: Enhances artistic expression, fine motor skills, and a connection with nature.

Variations: Paint rocks with different patterns or colors.

Bug and Insect Exploration

Description: While outdoors, observe and discuss insects and bugs you encounter with your toddler, encouraging curiosity and respect for nature.

Benefits: Fosters observation skills, empathy for insects, and a love for the outdoors.

Variations: Learn about different insect species.

Butterfly Watching

Description: Learn about butterflies and observe them in gardens or parks, discussing their colors and behavior with your toddler.

Benefits: Encourages observation skills, insect knowledge, and appreciation for nature's beauty.

Variations: Explore different butterfly species.

Outdoor Yoga and Relaxation

Description: Practice simple outdoor yoga and relaxation exercises with your toddler, connecting with nature and promoting mindfulness.

Benefits: Enhances body awareness, relaxation, and a connection with the natural environment.

Variations: Explore different yoga poses and relaxation techniques.

Music and Sound Activities

Birdsong Symphonies

Description: Listen to birdsongs and try to mimic them using your voices or simple instruments like whistles.

Benefits: Encourages auditory exploration, creativity, and an appreciation for birds.

Variations: Learn about different birds and their songs.

Musical Instrument Exploration

Description: Provide a variety of musical instruments for your toddler to explore and play, encouraging auditory exploration and creativity.

Benefits: Enhances rhythm, auditory discrimination, and fine motor skills.

Variations: Offer different musical instruments to experiment with.

Singing and Movement

Description: Sing songs with your toddler while incorporating movements like clapping, stomping, or dancing.

Benefits: Promotes language development, rhythm perception, and physical coordination.

Variations: Explore different songs and movements.

Musical Storytelling

Description: Create musical stories by narrating simple tales with background music or sound effects.

Benefits: Fosters imagination, language development, and music appreciation.

Variations: Create stories with different themes.

Nature's Symphony

Description: Listen to the sounds of nature like wind rustling through trees, waves crashing, or rain falling.

Benefits: Encourages auditory exploration, relaxation, and appreciation for the natural world.

Variations: Explore different natural soundscapes.

Sound Exploration with Natural Objects

Description: Collect natural objects like pinecones, leaves, or rocks and experiment with the sounds they make when tapped, shaken, or scraped.

Benefits: Enhances auditory perception, creativity, and exploration.

Variations: Discover different natural materials and their sounds.

Nature-Inspired Songs

Description: Sing songs related to nature and incorporate outdoor elements into your singing, like using leaves as makeshift instruments.

Benefits: Promotes language development, bonding, and a connection with nature.

Variations: Explore songs from different cultures or traditions.

Language and Communication Activities

Nature Vocabulary Cards

Description: Create vocabulary cards with pictures of natural objects (e.g., trees, animals, flowers) to expand your toddler's vocabulary.

Benefits: Enhances language development, word recognition, and nature appreciation.

Variations: Use cards with different themes.

Reading Aloud

Description: Read age-appropriate books aloud to your toddler, discussing the story and pictures to promote language development and comprehension.

Benefits: Enhances vocabulary, comprehension, and bonding.

Variations: Explore different books and themes.

Conversation with Nature

Description: Encourage your toddler to engage in conversations with natural elements during outdoor walks, like talking to a tree or a bird.

Benefits: Fosters imagination, language development, and a connection with nature.

Variations: Explore different aspects of nature to converse with.

Storytelling with Puppets

Description: Use hand puppets or stuffed animals to tell stories and encourage the child to participate in storytelling.

Benefits: Fosters language development, creativity, and imagination.

Variations: Create different story scenarios and characters.

Social, Bonding, and Emotional Development Activities

Outdoor Group Play

Description: Organize outdoor playdates with other toddlers to promote social interaction, sharing, and cooperation.

Benefits: Enhances social skills, communication, and friendship building.

Variations: Change activities and people to play with.

Nature Art Exhibition

Description: Organize a small outdoor art exhibition with your toddler's nature-inspired artwork for family and friends to admire.

Benefits: Fosters a sense of pride, confidence, and creativity.

Variations: Include other children's artwork as well.

Community Visits

Description: Plan visits to places like the library, fire station, or farmer's market to explore the community.

Benefits: Encourages social interaction, awareness of the world, and curiosity about the community.

Variations: Explore different community locations and discuss what they offer.

Indoor Fort Building

Description: Collaborate with your child to build indoor forts using blankets and cushions. Discuss cooperation and teamwork.

Benefits: Promotes teamwork, creativity, and imaginative play.

Variations: Experiment with different fort designs and uses.

Mindful Breathing with a Hug

Description: Practice mindful breathing together with your child, using a soft, comforting object to hug during deep breaths.

Benefits: Teaches emotional regulation, relaxation, and bonding.

Variations: Use a favorite stuffed animal or a cozy blanket.

Cognitive Development Activities

Color Mixing with Watercolors

Description: Allow the child to experiment with watercolors and explore color mixing.

Benefits: Enhances creativity, fine motor skills, and an understanding of color theory.

Variations: Experiment with different color combinations and painting techniques.

Memory Games

Description: Play simple memory games using cards with matching images and encourage the child to find the pairs.

Benefits: Enhances memory, concentration, and cognitive skills.

Variations: Increase the number of cards or introduce more complex images as the child's memory improves.

Block Stacking

Description: Offer a set of wooden or foam blocks and encourage your child to build towers and structures.

Benefits: Develops spatial awareness, problem-solving skills, and fine motor skills.

Variations: Introduce different block shapes and sizes.

Hand-Eye Coordination with Ball Play

Description: Engage in ball play, encouraging your child to catch, throw, and aim at targets.

Benefits: Enhances hand-eye coordination, motor skills, and spatial awareness.

Variations: Use different types of balls, set up targets, or try different throwing games.

Puzzles

Description: Offer age-appropriate puzzles with large pieces. Encourage your child to complete the puzzle, which aids in problem-solving and cognitive development.

Benefits: Enhances spatial awareness, hand-eye coordination, and logical thinking.

Variations: Choose puzzles with different themes or levels of complexity.

2 TO 3 YEARS

Practical Life Skills

Pouring Water

Description: Provide a small pitcher and a glass for your toddler to pour water into the glass.

Benefits: Develops hand-eye coordination, fine motor skills, and independence.

Variations: Use colored water for added visual appeal or containers of different sizes and shapes.

Dressing Skills

Description: Encourage your toddler to dress and undress independently, starting with simple items like shirts, socks, hats, weather boots.

Benefits: Fosters self-reliance, fine motor skills, and a sense of accomplishment.

Variation: Practice different types of clothing.

Table Setting

Description: Teach your toddler to set the table, placing utensils, plates, and cups in their proper places.

Benefits: Promotes orderliness, sequencing, and responsibility.

Variations: Use placemats with illustrations of where items should go.

Food Preparation

Description: Involve your toddler in age-appropriate food preparation tasks, like spreading butter on bread, slicing soft fruits.

Benefits: Enhances coordination, confidence, and a connection to food.

Variations: Explore different foods and preparation methods.

Plant Care

Description: Allow your toddler to care for a small potted plant by watering it and observing its growth.

Benefits: Nurtures responsibility, understanding of plant life, and a connection with nature.

Variations: Plant different types of plants.

Cleanup Practice

Description: Engage your toddler in daily cleanup activities like sweeping, dusting, or folding laundry to develop practical life skills.

Benefits: Builds independence, responsibility, and fine motor skills.

Variations: Explore various household tasks.

Cooking Together

Description: Involve your toddler in simple cooking activities like mixing, pouring, or rolling dough.

Benefits: Enhances culinary skills, understanding of food, and creativity.

Variations: Cook different recipes together.

Nature Cleanup

Description: Teach your toddler to clean up natural materials like leaves or sticks after outdoor play.

Benefits: Fosters responsibility, environmental awareness, and tidiness.

Variations: Clean up different outdoor play areas.

Buttoning and Snapping

Description: Introduce clothing items with buttons or snaps, allowing your toddler to practice fastening and unfastening.

Benefits: Develops fine motor skills, finger dexterity, and dressing independence.

Variations: Use clothes with different fasteners.

Cognitive Development Activities

Memory Card Games

Description: Play simple memory card games with matching pairs. This boosts memory skills and concentration.

Benefits: Enhances memory skills and concentration.

Variations: Add a scoring system with goals to reach.

Building Blocks Match

Description: Build simple structures with blocks and challenge your child to create the same structure.

Benefits: Enhances spatial awareness, problem-solving skills and concentration.

Variations: Vary the complexity of the structures to match the child's abilities.

Shape and Letter Tracing

Description: Introduce basic shape and letter tracing activities to prepare for writing and reading. Use large, easy-to-hold writing tools and guide your child's hand in tracing shapes and letters.

Benefits: Develops hand-eye coordination, fine-motor skills and concentration.

Variations: Use more complex shapes like animals or fruits and vegetables as the child progresses.

Puzzle play

Description: Provide age-appropriate puzzles with large, simple pieces.

Benefits: Develops observation, problem-solving and fine-motor skills.

Variations: Use more complex puzzles as the child progresses.

Building a Fort with Blankets

Description: Use blankets or sheets to create a fort. Encourage the child to help build and arrange the blankets.

Benefits: Stimulates creativity, spatial awareness and promotes cooperation and teamwork.

Variations: Add lighting elements or make a picnic inside the fort.

Sensory and Motor Skills Activities

Nature Sensory Walk

Description: Take a sensory nature walk, encouraging your toddler to touch leaves, smell flowers, and listen to the sounds of nature.

Benefits: Enhances sensory awareness, nature appreciation, and outdoor exploration.

Variations: Explore different outdoor environments.

Sensory Board

Description: Create a sensory board with various textured materials and safe interactive hardware pieces like locks, chains, gears, switches, etc.

Benefits: Develops tactile discrimination, sensory awareness, and fine motor skills.

Variations: Include different textures and materials.

Water and Sand Play

Description: Provide a water table or sandbox for children to explore and experiment with water, sand, and various tools.

Benefits: Enhances sensory exploration, fine motor skills, and creativity.

Variations: Add toys, molds, or natural elements like shells or pebbles.

Natural Playdough

Description: Make natural playdough using ingredients like flour, salt, and natural dyes for creative play.

Benefits: Enhances fine motor skills, creativity, and sensory exploration.

Variations: Experiment with scents and colors.

Scented Sensory Bins

Description: Fill sensory bins with scented materials like dried herbs, flowers, car freshners, essential oils on pieces of cloth, for olfactory exploration.

Benefits: Stimulates the sense of smell, sensory awareness, and relaxation.

Variations: Use different scents and materials.

Water Pouring with Precision

Description: Provide a pitcher and two glasses for your toddler to pour water accurately from one glass to another.

Benefits: Develops hand-eye coordination, fine motor skills, and concentration.

Variations: Use different-sized containers.

Obstacle Course

Description: Set up an indoor or outdoor obstacle course using cushions, tunnels, and cones, promoting physical activity and coordination.

Benefits: Enhances gross motor skills, balance, and spatial awareness.

Variations: Change the course layout for variety.

Language and Communication Activities

Montessori Sandpaper Letters

Description: Introduce Montessori sandpaper letters to help children learn letter shapes by touch. Encourage them to trace the letters.

Benefits: Enhances letter recognition, tactile exploration, and pre-reading skills.

Variations: Progress to more advanced letter materials.

DIY Story Cubes

Description: Create story cubes with images of different nature elements. Roll the cubes and create stories based on the images.

Benefits: Enhances storytelling skills, vocabulary development, and creativity.

Variations: Make story cubes with various themes or settings.

Storytime

Description: Read age-appropriate books to your toddler, discussing the story and asking open-ended questions.

Benefits: Promotes language development, vocabulary, and a love for reading.

Variations: Explore different genres of books.

Nature Vocabulary Cards

Description: Create vocabulary cards with pictures of natural objects (e.g., animals, plants) to expand your toddler's vocabulary.

Benefits: Enhances language development, word recognition, and nature appreciation.

Variations: Use cards with different themes.

Outdoor Storytelling

Description: Practice storytelling outdoors, taking turns to create imaginative tales based on the natural surroundings, fostering imagination and language development.

Benefits: Encourages creativity, language development, and a connection with nature.

Variations: Explore different storytelling themes.

Math and Numeracy Activities

Montessori Number Cards

Description: Introduce Montessori number cards with quantities represented by dots. Children can match the number to the quantity.

Benefits: Enhances number recognition, counting, and fine motor skills.

Variations: Progress to more advanced number cards.

Number Bean Sorting

Description: Provide children with a variety of beans or small objects to sort into containers based on numbers (e.g., place 3 beans in one container).

Benefits: Enhances counting, sorting, and fine motor skills.

Variations: Increase the number range as children develop their skills.

Nature Math

Description: Use natural materials like sticks, pebbles, or acorns for math activities. Children can practice counting, adding, or making simple patterns.

Benefits: Fosters numeracy, problem-solving, and a connection to nature.

Variations: Explore different math concepts and challenges.

Number Line Hopscotch

Description: Create a number line on the ground with chalk and play hopscotch. Children can jump on the numbers while counting.

Benefits: Promotes number recognition, counting skills, and physical activity.

Variations: Use hopscotch for basic addition or subtraction.

DIY Abacus

Description: Help children create a simple abacus using beads and string. They can use it to practice counting and simple addition.

Benefits: Promotes counting skills, understanding of quantities, and fine motor skills.

Variations: Experiment with different colors and sizes of beads.

Science and Nature Exploration

Nature Treasure Hunt

Description: Go on nature treasure hunts, searching for specific natural items (e.g., pinecones, rocks) and naming them.

Benefits: Improves vocabulary, observation skills, and outdoor exploration.

Variations: Focus on different categories of items.

Seed Planting

Description: Plant seeds in pots or a small garden, allowing your toddler to observe and care for the growing plants.

Benefits: Nurtures a love for gardening, responsibility, and understanding of plant life.

Variations: Plant different types of seeds.

Weather Observation Cards

Description: Discuss and observe different weather conditions with your toddler, and determine together which of the Weather Cards describes best the current conditions..

Benefits: Introduces weather concepts, observation skills, and scientific exploration.

Variations: Explore different weather patterns.

Bug Hotel Creation

Description: Build a bug hotel together using natural materials like sticks, leaves, and pinecones, providing shelter for insects in your garden, promoting empathy for insects and environmental awareness.

Benefits: Nurtures empathy for insects, environmental awareness, and construction skills.

Variations: Experiment with bug hotel designs.

Animal Tracks

Description: Search for animal tracks in mud or sand during nature walks, identifying the animals responsible.

Benefits: Enhances tracking skills, nature awareness, and understanding of animal behavior.

Variations: Explore different animal tracks.

Nature Collections

Description: Go on nature walks with your toddler to collect and document interesting natural items like leaves, rocks, or shells.

Benefits: Fosters a connection with nature, observation skills, and an appreciation for the outdoors.

Variations: Create themed nature collections.

Planting a Butterfly Garden

Description: Plant butterfly-friendly flowers and plants in your garden or pots, learning about plant care and attracting butterflies, nurturing a love for gardening and responsibility.

Benefits: Nurtures a love for gardening, responsibility, and awareness of the ecosystem.

Variations: Choose different butterfly-attracting plants.

DIY Science Experiments

Description: Conduct simple science experiments, like creating a volcano with baking soda and vinegar or making a vortex taping together two plastic bottles half-filled with coloured water.

Benefits: Enhances curiosity, problem-solving, and basic scientific understanding.

Variations: Explore a variety of age-appropriate science experiments.

DIY Mini Greenhouse

Description: Create a small greenhouse together with clear plastic containers to grow seeds or plants indoors.

Benefits: Teaches plant growth, responsibility, and an understanding of ecosystems.

Variations: Experiment with different types of seeds or plants.

Arts and Crafts Activities

Leaf Rubbings

Description: Collect leaves of different shapes and textures and create leaf rubbings using crayons and paper, fostering creativity and exploration.

Benefits: Enhances fine motor skills, texture exploration, and appreciation for leaf diversity.

Variations: Explore leaves with various colors and sizes.

Nature Shadow Art

Description: Experiment with creating art using natural objects and sunlight or spotlight to cast shadows, promoting artistic expression and creativity.

Benefits: Enhances fine motor skills, creativity, and understanding of light and shadow.

Variations: Explore different objects and angles for shadow art.

Nature Collages

Description: Collect natural materials like leaves, petals, and twigs to create collages with glue and paper.

Benefits: Fosters creativity, fine motor skills, and an appreciation for nature's textures.

Variations: Create themed collages.

Recycled Art Projects

Description: Provide a collection of recyclable materials (e.g., cardboard, bottle caps) for children to create sculptures, collages, or functional art.

Benefits: Fosters creativity, fine motor skills, and environmental awareness.

Variations: Explore different recycled materials and art projects.

Bead Stringing

Description: Provide large beads and strings for children to practice threading. They can create necklaces or bracelets.

Benefits: Fosters fine motor skills, hand-eye coordination, and concentration.

Variations: Use beads of different sizes or introduce patterns.

Paper Collage

Description: Provide colored paper and glue. Children can tear and glue the paper to create colorful collages.

Benefits: Enhances creativity, fine motor skills, and color recognition.

Variations: Explore different collage themes.

Nature Printing

Description: Collect leaves, flowers, pinecones, or tree bark. Dip them in paint and use them to create prints on paper or fabric.

Benefits: Fosters creativity, fine motor skills, and an appreciation for nature.

Variations: Experiment with different natural materials and printing surfaces.

Music and Sound Activities

Montessori Sound Cylinders

Description: Introduce Montessori sound cylinders with pairs of containers that make matching sounds. Encourage children to match the sounds.

Benefits: Enhances auditory discrimination, sound recognition, and concentration.

Variations: Progress to more complex sound cylinders.

Homemade Shakers

Description: Help children create their own shakers using small containers filled with rice, beans, or pasta. Encourage them to shake and make music.

Benefits: Fosters creativity, fine motor skills, and an understanding of cause and effect.

Variations: Experiment with different fillings for the shakers or decorate them.

Outdoor Drum Circle

Description: Arrange an outdoor drum circle with simple hand drums, buckets, or pans. Let children explore rhythm and make music together.

Benefits: Promotes rhythm awareness, social interaction, and physical activity.

Variations: Use various percussion instruments or introduce rhythmic patterns.

Nature Sound Jars

Description: Create sound jars by filling clear containers with natural materials like stones, shells, or pinecones. Children can shake and compare the sounds.

Benefits: Enhances auditory discrimination, sensory exploration, and language development.

Variations: Use different natural materials for the sound jars.

Music with Everyday Objects

Description: Encourage children to make music using everyday objects like pots, pans, wooden spoons, or empty plastic bottles.

Benefits: Promotes creativity, fine motor skills, and imaginative play.

Variations: Explore different objects and create "music ensembles."

DIY Xylophone

Description: Help children create a simple xylophone using glasses or bottles filled with varying amounts of water. They can experiment with different notes.

Benefits: Fosters an understanding of pitch, fine motor skills, and experimentation.

Variations: Use containers of different sizes for more notes.

3 TO 4 YEARS

Arts and Crafts Activities

Stringing Beads

Description: Offer beads and strings for preschoolers to string, creating necklaces or bracelets.

Benefits: Enhances fine motor skills, concentration, and creativity.

Variations: Use beads of different shapes and sizes.

Nature Weaving

Description: Use natural materials like twigs, leaves, and yarn to weave simple patterns or designs.

Benefits: Enhances fine motor skills, creativity, and an appreciation for nature's materials.

Variations: Experiment with different weaving patterns.

Nature Art and Sculptures

Description: Encourage preschoolers to create art and sculptures using natural materials like sticks, leaves, and stones.

Benefits: Fosters creativity, fine motor skills, and a connection to nature.

Variations: Experiment with different natural materials.

Nature Collages with Shapes

Description: Collect natural materials like leaves and create collages using predefined shapes.

Benefits: Fosters creativity, fine motor skills, and shape recognition.

Variations: Use different natural materials.

Nature Mandalas

Description: Use natural objects like flowers, leaves, and stones to create mandala designs.

Benefits: Enhances fine motor skills, creativity, and an appreciation for symmetry.

Variations: Explore different mandala patterns.

Practical Life Skills Activities

Folding Laundry

Description: Teach preschoolers to fold their own clothes, starting with simple items like washcloths and gradually progressing to larger ones.

Benefits: Enhances fine motor skills, concentration, and a sense of responsibility.

Variations: Include different types of clothing.

Simple Cooking

Description: Involve preschoolers in basic cooking tasks such as mixing, pouring, or spreading, under close supervision.

Benefits: Develops cooking skills, independence, and an understanding of food preparation.

Variations: Try age-appropriate recipes.

Planting Seeds and Garden Care

Description: Encourage preschoolers to plant seeds, care for a garden, and observe plant growth.

Benefits: Nurtures an understanding of plant biology, responsibility, and a connection to nature.

Variations: Plant different types of seeds or plants.

Sock Matching

Description: Mix up pairs of socks and have preschoolers match them by size, color, or pattern.

Benefits: Enhances fine motor skills, concentration, and the ability to recognize patterns.

Variations: Use different types of clothing items.

Table Setting for Meals

Description: Teach preschoolers how to set the table properly for meals, including arranging plates, utensils, and napkins.

Benefits: Promotes independence, responsibility, and mealtime etiquette.

Variations: Set the table for different meal types (breakfast, lunch, dinner).

Plant Care and Watering

Description: Assign preschoolers the responsibility of caring for indoor plants, including watering and observing growth.

Benefits: Nurtures a sense of responsibility, plant knowledge, and a connection to nature.

Variations: Care for different types of indoor plants.

Button Sorting

Description: Provide a variety of buttons and encourage preschoolers to sort them by size, color, or shape.

Benefits: Enhances fine motor skills, sorting abilities, and attention to detail.

Variations: Use different small objects for sorting.

Snack Preparation

Description: Involve preschoolers in making simple snacks like fruit kabobs or sandwiches with age-appropriate tasks.

Benefits: Enhances food preparation skills, independence, and an understanding of nutrition.

Variations: Experiment with different snack recipes.

Water Pouring and Transferring

Description: Provide water and small containers for preschoolers to practice pouring and transferring.

Benefits: Develops hand-eye coordination, concentration, and independence.

Variations: Use different containers and liquids.

Table Manners Practice

Description: Teach preschoolers proper table manners, including using utensils, napkin placement, and chewing with mouths closed.

Benefits: Develops etiquette, independence, and social skills.

Variations: Have a pretend tea party to practice manners.

Shoe Tying

Description: Teach preschoolers how to tie their shoes, focusing on bunny ears or other easy techniques.

Benefits: Enhances fine motor skills and independence.

Variations: Use shoes with different fastening methods.

Bed Making

Description: Show preschoolers how to make their beds neatly with proper tucking and folding.

Benefits: Promotes orderliness and responsibility.

Variations: Create a bed-making checklist.

Planting and Gardening

Description: Involve preschoolers in planting and caring for flowers or vegetables in a garden.

Benefits: Nurtures a love for nature, responsibility, and plant knowledge.

Variations: Plant different types of plants.

Cleaning Up Independently

Description: Teach preschoolers to clean up their play area and put away toys and materials.

Benefits: Promotes responsibility, orderliness, and independence.

Variations: Create a cleanup checklist.

Washing Hands Independently

Description: Teach preschoolers to wash their hands properly, emphasizing soap and water use.

Benefits: Promotes hygiene, independence, and fine motor skills.

Variations: Use different soap scents or handwashing songs.

Dressing Themselves

Description: Encourage preschoolers to dress themselves, focusing on zipping, buttoning, and putting on shoes or boots.

Benefits: Develops self-sufficiency, fine motor skills, and self-confidence.

Variations: Practice dressing for different weather conditions.

Sensory and Fine Motor Activities

Scented Sensory Bottles

Description: Together, create sensory bottles filled with scented materials like herbs, spices, or flowers for sensory exploration.

Benefits: Stimulates the sense of smell, concentration, and sensory awareness.

Variations: Use various scented materials.

Threading and Lacing Cards

Description: Provide threading cards with holes for preschoolers to practice threading and lacing with yarn or shoelaces.

Benefits: Develops fine motor skills, hand-eye coordination, and patience.

Variations: Use different threading cards.

Sensory Bins with Letters and Numbers

Description: Create sensory bins with materials like rice or beans and hide letters and numbers for recognition and counting.

Benefits: Stimulates sensory perception, letter and number recognition, and fine motor skills.

Variations: Use different sensory materials.

Playdough Creations with Patterns and Shapes

Description: Provide playdough for preschoolers to create patterns and shapes.

Benefits: Enhances fine motor skills, creativity, and mathematical thinking.

Variations: Explore different patterns and shapes.

Scented Playdough

Description: Make scented playdough using natural ingredients like herbs or flowers for sensory play.

Benefits: Stimulates the sense of smell, creativity, and fine motor skills.

Variations: Use different scents and colors.

Sensory Board

Description: Create a sensory board with various textured materials and safe interactive hardware pieces like locks, chains, gears, switches, etc.

Benefits: Develops tactile discrimination, sensory awareness, and fine motor skills.

Variations: Include different textures and materials.

Language and Communication Activities

Storytelling with Puppets and Props

Description: Encourage preschoolers to create stories using puppets and props.

Benefits: Enhances language development, storytelling skills, and creativity.

Variations: Create different puppet characters for different settings.

Letter Sound Matching Game

Description: Match objects or images with their initial letter sounds to reinforce phonics.

Benefits: Develops phonemic awareness, letter-sound association, and vocabulary.

Variations: Focus on specific letter sounds.

Nature Story Stones

Description: Paint or draw images of natural objects on stones and use them to create nature-themed stories.

Benefits: Enhances language development, storytelling skills, and creativity.

Variations: Create story stones with different themes.

Nature Alphabet Scavenger Hunt

Description: Organize scavenger hunts where preschoolers find natural objects that represent each letter of the alphabet.

Benefits: Promotes letter recognition, vocabulary, and a connection to nature.

Variations: Focus on specific letters or habitats.

Word Building with Magnetic Letters

Description: Use magnetic letters to build words and simple sentences on a magnetic board.

Benefits: Develops literacy skills, spelling, and vocabulary.

Variations: Explore different word families and sentence structures.

Picture Books and Storytelling

Description: Read picture books together and encourage preschoolers to create their own stories based on the illustrations.

Benefits: Enhances language development, storytelling skills, and creativity.

Variations: Explore books from various genres.

Math and Numeracy Activities

Counting with Natural Objects

Description: Collect natural objects like pinecones or acorns and use them for counting and math activities.

Benefits: Enhances counting skills, number recognition, and mathematical understanding.

Variations: Count different types of natural objects.

Measuring and Comparing

Description: Use simple measuring tools like rulers or tape measures to compare and measure objects.

Benefits: Introduces measurement concepts, comparison skills, and mathematical thinking.

Variations: Explore different objects and measurement units.

Money Counting and Play Store

Description: Create a play store with pretend money for preschoolers to practice counting and making purchases.

Benefits: Develops basic math skills, money awareness, and role-play abilities.

Variations: Add price tags to items or change the currency.

Nature Patterns and Geometry

Description: Explore patterns and geometry in nature by examining leaves, flowers, and natural objects.

Benefits: Enhances pattern recognition, symmetry understanding, and appreciation for natural beauty.

Variations: Collect various natural objects to study patterns.

Shape Recognition and Building

Description: Introduce geometric shapes and encourage preschoolers to build structures using these shapes.

Benefits: Enhances shape recognition, spatial skills, and creative problem-solving.

Variations: Explore different shapes and create increasingly complex structures.

Number Games and Math Puzzles

Description: Play number games and solve math puzzles that involve counting, addition, and subtraction.

Benefits: Develops numeracy skills, problem-solving abilities, and mathematical thinking.

Variations: Explore different math concepts and levels of difficulty.

Pattern Making with Colors

Description: Create patterns using colored materials like beads or buttons.

Benefits: Enhances pattern recognition, sequencing, and color awareness.

Variations: Experiment with different colors and shapes.

Science and Nature Exploration Activities

Volcano Experiment

Description: Build a volcano using paper mâché and paint, then conduct a basic volcano experiment using baking soda and vinegar to demonstrate a volcanic eruption.

Benefits: Sparks scientific curiosity, introduces basic chemical reactions, and encourages hands-on learning.

Variations: Explore different volcano shapes using different materials like sand, moss, soil or rocks.

Cloud Watching and Identification

Description: Lie on a grassy area and watch clouds, identifying different cloud types and discussing weather.

Benefits: Encourages cloud and weather observation, curiosity, and scientific interest.

Variations: Explore different cloud formations.

Seasonal Observations and Art

Description: Observe and discuss changes in the seasons and create seasonal-themed art projects.

Benefits: Teaches about the natural world, seasons, and creativity.

Variations: Explore different seasonal art techniques.

Bird Watching and Identification

Description: Set up bird feeders and watch for different bird species, identifying them using field guides.

Benefits: Fosters an appreciation for wildlife, observation skills, and an understanding of bird behavior.

Variations: Focus on specific types of birds.

Seed Germination Experiment

Description: Conduct a simple seed germination experiment to show how plants grow from seeds. Put various seeds in different wet paper tissues and observe how the germination process over the next few days.

Benefits: Nurtures an understanding of plant biology and scientific curiosity.

Variations: Try different types of seeds.

Plant Life Cycle and Gardening

Description: Teach preschoolers about the life cycle of plants and involve them in gardening activities.

Benefits: Nurtures an understanding of plant biology, responsibility, and a love for gardening.

Variations: Plant different types of plants and explore various stages of the plant life cycle.

Nature Scavenger Hunt

Description: Organize nature scavenger hunts, where preschoolers search for specific natural items like pinecones or feathers.

Benefits: Fosters observation skills, connection to nature, and a sense of adventure.

Variations: Change the items to find or explore different outdoor locations.

Weather Chart and Observations

Description: Create a weather chart and have preschoolers observe and record daily weather.

Benefits: Introduces weather concepts, observation skills, and scientific exploration.

Variations: Explore different weather patterns.

Bug Hotel Creation

Description: Build a bug hotel together using natural materials like sticks, leaves, and pinecones, providing shelter for insects in your garden, promoting empathy for insects and environmental awareness.

Benefits: Nurtures empathy for insects, environmental awareness, and construction skills.

Variations: Experiment with bug hotel designs.

Geography and Cultural Activities

Around the World Cookbook

Description: Explore cuisines from different countries by cooking meals inspired by various cultures.

Benefits: Encourages cultural awareness, culinary skills, and a global perspective.

Variations: Focus on dishes from specific regions.

World Geography Puzzle

Description: Introduce preschoolers to world geography by assembling puzzles with maps of continents and countries.

Benefits: Promotes geographic awareness, problem-solving, and map-reading skills.

Variations: Use puzzles of different regions or landmarks.

Map Reading and Treasure Hunt

Description: Teach preschoolers basic map-reading skills by creating treasure maps and going on treasure hunts.

Benefits: Promotes spatial awareness, problem-solving, and a sense of adventure.

Variations: Create different treasure hunt scenarios.

Cultural Dress-Up and Celebration Day

Description: Explore cultures from around the world by dressing up in traditional clothing and exploring their cultural celebration customs through books, stories and activities.

Benefits: Encourages cultural awareness, respect for diversity, and imaginative play.

Variations: Focus on specific cultures and their attire.

Maps and Globes Exploration

Description: Introduce maps, globes, and atlases to teach basic geography concepts, including continents and countries.

Benefits: Promotes geographic awareness, map-reading skills, and global understanding.

Variations: Explore maps of different regions and continents.

Maps and Landforms

Description: Introduce maps and explore different landforms like mountains and rivers.

Benefits: Promotes geographic awareness and understanding of the world.

Variations: Explore maps of different regions.

4 TO 5 YEARS

Science and Nature Exploration Activities

Nature Scavenger Hunt

Description: Organize scavenger hunts in natural settings, encouraging children to find and identify specific objects or species.

Benefits: Stimulates observation skills, nature appreciation, and problem-solving.

Variations: Focus on different themes or ecosystems.

Solar System Exploration

Description: Learn about the solar system by creating a model, discussing planets, and exploring the concept of space.

Benefits: Fosters an interest in astronomy, scientific knowledge, and understanding of the solar system.

Variations: Explore different aspects of space.

Environmental Conservation Project

Description: Collaborate on a conservation project, such as planting trees or cleaning up a local park, discussing the importance of conservation.

Benefits: Promotes environmental awareness, a sense of responsibility, and community engagement.

Variations: Participate in different conservation projects.

Microscopic World Exploration

Description: Use microscopes to explore the microscopic world, discussing microorganisms and the importance of microscopic life.

Benefits: Enhances scientific curiosity, observation skills, and understanding of the micro world.

Variations: Explore different microscopic specimens.

Water Erosion Experiment

Description: Conduct a simple experiment to demonstrate how water erosion shapes landscapes, such as running water down a small trench in the sand on the beach.

Benefits: Sparks curiosity about geology, introduces erosion concepts, and encourages experimentation.

Variations: Experiment with different erosion scenarios.

Plant Propagation

Description: Explore plant propagation techniques, including seed sowing, cuttings, and grafting.

Benefits: Sparks curiosity about plant biology, gardening skills, and a love for greenery.

Variations: Propagate different plant species.

Physics of Flight

Description: Explore the physics of flight by creating paper airplanes, kites, and other flying objects.

Benefits: Encourages scientific curiosity, introduces physics concepts, and encourages experimentation.

Variations: Experiment with different flying designs.

Astronomy Nights

Description: Explore the night sky by observing stars, planets, and constellations during stargazing sessions.

Benefits: Fosters an interest in astronomy, scientific curiosity, and night sky awareness.

Variations: Focus on different celestial events.

Nature Classification

Description: Study classification by categorizing natural objects into groups based on specific criteria.

Benefits: Enhances classification skills, scientific thinking, and observation.

Variations: Classify different sets of natural objects.

Weather Observations

Description: Keep a weather journal, recording daily observations and discussing weather patterns.

Benefits: Encourages scientific curiosity, weather understanding, and data collection.

Variations: Track weather for different seasons.

Insect Study

Description: Explore the world of insects by observing, identifying, and learning about their habitats and behavior.

Benefits: Fosters curiosity, insect knowledge, and observation skills.

Variations: Focus on specific types of insects.

Arts and Crafts Activities

Nature Collage

Description: Gather a variety of natural materials like leaves, twigs, flowers, and pebbles. Provide children with paper and glue to create a collage using these materials.

Benefits: Encourages observation of nature, artistic expression, fine motor skills, and understanding of the environment.

Variations: Use different themes like underwater, jungle, or seasons to vary the collage materials.

Sensory Paint Exploration

Description: Prepare homemade sensory paints by mixing flour, water, and food coloring. Children can use their fingers, brushes, or sponges to paint and explore textures.

Benefits: Enhances sensory perception, creativity, fine motor skills, and color recognition.

Variations: Experiment with different textures, such as adding sand for a grainy texture or using scented paint for olfactory stimulation.

String Art

Description: Provide a piece of wood, nails, and colorful threads. Children can create geometric patterns or their own designs by wrapping the thread around the nails.

Benefits: Promotes concentration, hand-eye coordination, and geometric understanding.

Variations: Change the base material to cardboard or use different shapes like animals or letters as a base.

Seed Mosaic

Description: Offer a variety of seeds (e.g., lentils, beans, and rice) and glue. Children can create beautiful mosaic designs on cardboard using these seeds.

Benefits: Encourages fine motor skills, patience, and introduces the concept of patterns.

Variations: Use colored seeds, arrange the seeds to create specific shapes or patterns, or create a larger project over time.

Clay Sculptures

Description: Provide soft, moldable clay for sculpting. Children can use their imagination to create sculptures, animals, or abstract designs.

Benefits: Develops fine motor skills, 3D spatial awareness, and fosters creativity.

Variations: Try different types of clay, such as air-dry or polymer clay, or introduce sculpting tools for more intricate designs.

Leaf and Flower Pressing

Description: Collect leaves and flowers. Place them between sheets of paper and press them in a heavy book. After a few days, use these pressed leaves and flowers to create art.

Benefits: Teaches patience, observation, and appreciation for nature's beauty.

Variations: Experiment with different types of paper, or create greeting cards and bookmarks with the pressed materials.

Recycled Material Sculptures

Description: Collect recyclable materials like cardboard, plastic bottles, and egg cartons. Provide child-safe scissors and glue to create sculptures from these items.

Benefits: Encourages creativity, environmental awareness, and fine motor skills.

Variations: Use specific recyclable items to create a themed sculpture, such as making a robot from old boxes.

Sandpaper Art

Description: Place sandpaper beneath a piece of plain paper and let children rub crayons or pastels over it to create textured drawings.

Benefits: Enhances sensory exploration, fine motor skills, and introduces texture concepts.

Variations: Use different grades of sandpaper for varying textures or try this technique with different coloring tools like watercolors or oil pastels.

Bead Threading

Description: Provide beads and strings. Children can thread the beads to create necklaces or bracelets.

Benefits: Develops hand-eye coordination, fine motor skills, and pattern recognition.

Variations: Use different shapes and colors of beads, or introduce letter beads for spelling practice.

Torn Paper Collage

Description: Offer a variety of colored papers and encourage children to tear and glue the paper pieces to create pictures and designs.

Benefits: Enhances fine motor skills, creativity, and understanding of shapes and textures.

Variations: Experiment with different paper types, such as tissue paper, magazine cutouts, or wrapping paper.

Yarn Knitting

Description: Teach children to finger knit using yarn. They can create scarves, headbands, or simple bracelets.

Benefits: Enhances fine motor skills, hand coordination, and patience.

Variations: Experiment with different yarn types and colors, or guide children in creating more complex knitting patterns.

Leaf Rubbings

Description: Collect leaves from various trees. Place a leaf under a sheet of paper and rub a crayon over it to create leaf imprints.

Benefits: Teaches observation, fine motor skills, and introduces children to the diversity of nature.

Variations: Explore different types of leaves, create a leaf identification book, or incorporate the rubbings into larger art projects.

Shadow Art

Description: Set up a table with a strong light source and various objects like toys or figures. Children can create art by tracing the shadows of these objects on paper.

Benefits: Encourages observation, understanding of light and shadow, and creativity.

Variations: Experiment with different light angles and objects to create diverse shadow art.

Rock Painting

Description: Collect smooth, flat rocks and provide paint and brushes. Children can paint imaginative designs or creatures on the rocks.

Benefits: Enhances creativity, fine motor skills, and an appreciation for nature.

Variations: Paint rocks with themes like animals, insects, or inspirational messages. You can also varnish the rocks for a glossy finish.

Nature Dyeing

Description: Gather flowers, leaves, and berries. Children can use these natural materials to dye fabric or paper.

Benefits: Encourages an appreciation for nature, creativity, and introduces the concept of color blending.

Variations: Experiment with different fabrics and materials, or create unique designs using different combinations of natural dyes.

Sculpture Garden

Description: Provide children with clay and encourage them to sculpt small figurines. Create a miniature sculpture garden by placing these sculptures in a designated area.

Benefits: Develops fine motor skills, encourages creativity, and fosters an appreciation for art.

Variations: Consider adding natural elements like pebbles, small plants, or shells to the sculpture garden for a unique touch.

Yarn-Wrapped Letters

Description: Write letters or words on pieces of cardboard. Children can wrap colorful yarn around these letters to create textured, tactile art.

Benefits: Enhances fine motor skills, letter recognition, and introduces early literacy concepts.

Variations: Customize this activity based on the child's name or favorite words. Experiment with different colors and types of yarn.

Homemade Musical Instruments

Description: Encourage children to make simple musical instruments like shakers using empty containers and dried beans, or drums using empty coffee cans.

Benefits: Fosters creativity, rhythm, and an understanding of sound and music.

Variations: Experiment with different materials and sizes to create a variety of homemade instruments, such as tambourines or rainsticks.

Patterned Nature Prints

Description: Collect leaves, flowers, and other natural materials. Children can dip these items in paint and create patterned prints on paper or fabric.

Benefits: Encourages an appreciation for nature, introduces patterns, and fosters creativity.

Variations: Use different colored paints or experiment with various printing surfaces like canvas or fabric.

Fruit and Vegetable Stamps

Description: Cut fruits and vegetables like apples, potatoes, and celery in half. Dip these in paint and use them as stamps to create artwork.

Benefits: Introduces different textures and shapes, enhances creativity, and teaches about fruits and vegetables.

Variations: Try different fruits and vegetables to create diverse stamp patterns and artwork.

Origami

Description: Provide children with square pieces of paper and teach them simple origami folds to create various paper animals, flowers, or shapes.

Benefits: Enhances fine motor skills, patience, and introduces geometry concepts.

Variations: Start with basic origami designs and gradually progress to more complex ones as children become more skilled.

Collaborative Mural Painting

Description: Provide a large sheet of paper or cardboard and let children collaborate on a mural by painting together.

Benefits: Fosters teamwork, creativity, and allows children to express themselves in a group project.

Variations: Theme the mural based on children's interests or the season, or use various painting techniques like finger painting or splatter painting.

Practical Life Skills Activities

Basic Electrical Knowledge

Description: Introduce children to basic electrical knowledge, teaching them about electrical outlets, plugs, and safety.

Benefits: Promotes safety awareness, practical skills, and understanding of electricity.

Variations: Explore different electrical appliances.

Basic Car Maintenance

Description: Teach children basic car maintenance skills, such as checking tire pressure and oil levels.

Benefits: Promotes safety, practical skills, and understanding of vehicle maintenance.

Variations: Explore different aspects of car care.

Planting and Harvesting

Description: Continue exploring gardening by involving children in the planting and harvesting of vegetables or fruits.

Benefits: Nurtures an understanding of food production, responsibility, and sustainability.

Variations: Grow different types of crops.

Basic First Aid

Description: Teach children basic first-aid skills like applying band-aids, cleaning and disinfecting minor cuts and scrapes.

Benefits: Promotes safety, self-reliance, and preparedness in emergencies.

Variations: Practice different first-aid techniques.

Organizing a Closet

Description: Involve children in organizing their own closet, arranging clothes by type, season, or color.

Benefits: Develops organization skills, independence, and a sense of order.

Variations: Organize different sections of the closet.

Basic Woodworking

Description: Introduce children to basic woodworking with age-appropriate tools to create simple wooden projects.

Benefits: Fosters craftsmanship, fine motor skills, and creativity.

Variations: Explore different woodworking projects.

Basic Sewing

Description: Teach children basic sewing skills using child-safe needles, fabric, and simple stitching techniques.

Benefits: Enhances fine motor skills, patience, and introduces a practical skill.

Variations: Create simple sewing projects like a felt ornament.

Shoe Tying

Description: Teach preschoolers how to tie their shoes, starting with simple knots and progressing to shoelaces.

Benefits: Enhances fine motor skills, independence, and self-care abilities.

Variations: Practice with different types of shoelaces.

Cooking Meals

Description: Involve preschoolers in more complex cooking tasks, such as measuring ingredients and following recipes.

Benefits: Develops cooking skills, math concepts, and an appreciation for food preparation.

Variations: Explore diverse cuisines and dishes.

Self-Setting Table

Description: Teach preschoolers to set the table independently, including arranging plates, utensils, and cups.

Benefits: Promotes independence, fine motor skills, and mealtime etiquette.

Variations: Set the table for different meals or occasions.

Dishwashing

Description: Involve preschoolers in washing dishes, starting with non-breakable items and gradually progressing to more delicate ones.

Benefits: Develops responsibility, hand-eye coordination, and practical life skills.

Variations: Use different types of dishes and utensils.

Plant Care and Gardening

Description: Assign preschoolers the responsibility of caring for a garden, including planting, weeding, and harvesting.

Benefits: Nurtures an understanding of plant biology, responsibility, and a connection to nature.

Variations: Plant different types of vegetables or flowers.

Sensory and Fine Motor Activities

Building with Blocks

Description: Encourage children to build structures using wooden blocks, promoting creativity and problem-solving.

Benefits: Enhances spatial awareness, fine motor skills, and imaginative play.

Variations: Build different types of structures.

Aromatherapy with Herbs

Description: Explore aromatherapy by drying and using herbs to create scented sachets or potpourri.

Benefits: Enhances sensory perception, relaxation, and an understanding of scents.

Variations: Experiment with different herbs and scents.

Nature Photography

Description: Introduce children to photography by allowing them to take pictures of the natural world and discussing their observations.

Benefits: Develops observation skills, creativity, and an appreciation for photography.

Variations: Explore different photography themes.

Texture Exploration Book

Description: Create a tactile exploration book with pages featuring various textures for children to touch and describe.

Benefits: Enhances sensory perception, vocabulary, and fine motor skills.

Variations: Include different textures and materials.

String Art

Description: Explore string art by using pins, strings, and a corkboard to create geometric patterns or images.

Benefits: Fosters creativity, fine motor skills, and an understanding of geometry.

Variations: Experiment with different designs and colors.

Pottery and Clay Sculpting

Description: Introduce pottery and clay sculpting, allowing children to create three-dimensional art.

Benefits: Fosters creativity, fine motor skills, and an understanding of sculptural art.

Variations: Experiment with different clay types and techniques.

Nature Weaving

Description: Use natural materials like long grasses or twigs to create simple weaving projects.

Benefits: Enhances fine motor skills, creativity, and an appreciation for natural materials.

Variations: Explore different weaving patterns.

Nature Art with Found Objects

Description: Use natural objects like sticks, leaves, and stones to create sculptures or collages.

Benefits: Enhances creativity, fine motor skills, and an appreciation for nature's materials.

Variations: Explore different art forms and themes.

Threading and Beading

Description: Provide beads and strings for preschoolers to thread and create jewelry or patterns.

Benefits: Enhances fine motor skills, concentration, and creativity.

Variations: Use beads of different shapes and materials.

Language and Communication Activities

Mime Time

Description: Fill a bowl with names of animals, characters or people on pieces of paper and take turns at picking a name and trying to make the other person guess the animal by imitating in silence.

Benefits: Enhances creativity, problem-solving and teamwork.

Variations: Use a hourglass and guess as many animals, characters or people as possible within a certain timeframe.

Nature-inspired Storytelling

Description: Encourage children to create stories inspired by nature, using elements like animals, trees, and landscapes.

Benefits: Enhances storytelling skills, language development, and imagination.

Variations: Explore different natural themes.

Bilingual Learning

Description: Introduce children to a new language, promoting bilingualism through songs, stories, and basic conversations.

Benefits: Enhances language development, cognitive skills, and cultural awareness.

Variations: Explore different languages.

Creative Storytelling

Description: Encourage children to create and illustrate their own stories, fostering storytelling skills and artistic expression.

Benefits: Enhances narrative abilities, creativity, and fine motor skills.

Variations: Explore different story genres.

Storytelling with Puppets

Description: Encourage preschoolers to create and perform puppet shows, developing storytelling skills and creativity.

Benefits: Enhances language development, imagination, and dramatic play.

Variations: Create puppet characters for different stories.

Reading Comprehension

Description: Read age-appropriate books and engage preschoolers in discussions about the story, characters, and lessons.

Benefits: Enhances comprehension skills, vocabulary, and critical thinking.

Variations: Explore books from different genres and cultures.

Math and Numeracy Activities

Nature-inspired Geometry

Description: Explore geometry concepts using natural objects, discussing shapes, angles, and symmetry.

Benefits: Develops geometry understanding, math skills, and observation.

Variations: Explore different geometric concepts.

Fraction Exploration

Description: Introduce children to fractions using natural objects like fruits or shapes to illustrate fractions.

Benefits: Develops understanding of fractions, math skills, and problem-solving.

Variations: Explore different fractions.

Money Math Challenges

Description: Create money-related math challenges where children solve problems involving addition, subtraction, and money calculations.

Benefits: Develops financial literacy, math skills, and problem-solving.

Variations: Explore different math challenges.

Time-telling with Sundials

Description: Learn about time-telling by creating and using simple sundials in an outdoor setting.

Benefits: Promotes time awareness, an understanding of sundials, and observational skills.

Variations: Explore sundials in different locations.

Math Story Problems

Description: Create math story problems based on real-life situations and encourage children to solve them.

Benefits: Develops math skills, problem-solving abilities, and mathematical reasoning.

Variations: Explore different math concepts.

Calendar Math

Description: Engage in calendar-related math activities, such as calculating days between dates or identifying patterns.

Benefits: Enhances calendar skills, math concepts, and logical thinking.

Variations: Create calendar-based challenges.

Money Management

Description: Introduce children to basic money management, including saving, spending, and budgeting for small expenses.

Benefits: Develops financial literacy, math skills, and responsibility.

Variations: Explore different financial scenarios.

Calendar Activities

Description: Teach children about calendars, days of the week, months, and special events through calendar-related activities like a DIY chocolate Advent calendar.

Benefits: Promotes time awareness, calendar skills, and organization.

Variations: Create themed calendars.

Counting Collections

Description: Collect objects from nature like leaves or rocks and practice counting and grouping them.

Benefits: Develops counting skills, number recognition, and basic math concepts.

Variations: Count different types of natural objects.

Shape Scavenger Hunt

Description: Organize shape-themed scavenger hunts in nature, searching for objects that match specific shapes.

Benefits: Enhances shape recognition, geometry understanding, and observation skills.

Variations: Focus on different shapes.

Geography and Cultural Activities

Mapping Adventures

Description: Go on mapping adventures where children use maps to navigate and explore different locations.

Benefits: Promotes map-reading skills, geographic awareness, and exploration.

Variations: Explore different maps and destinations.

World Flags

Description: Learn about flags from around the world, discussing their symbolism and the countries they represent.

Benefits: Encourages cultural awareness, flag recognition, and a global perspective.

Variations: Explore flags from different continents.

Cultural Cooking Experiments

Description: Conduct cooking experiments by recreating traditional dishes from different cultures, discussing their ingredients and history.

Benefits: Encourages cultural appreciation, culinary skills, and global awareness.

Variations: Explore dishes from specific countries.

World Geography Board Game

Description: Play a geography-themed board game that explores world countries, landmarks, and cultural facts.

Benefits: Promotes geographic awareness, critical thinking, and global knowledge.

Variations: Try different geography board games.

Cultural Festivals

Description: Explore cultural festivals from around the world, discussing their traditions, music, food, and celebrations.

Benefits: Encourages cultural appreciation, global awareness, and a sense of celebration.

Variations: Explore festivals from different Continents

Puzzle Map

Description: Learn about continents by using puzzle maps to identify and place continents in their correct locations.

Benefits: Promotes geographic awareness, spatial understanding, and world geography.

Variations: Explore different aspects of continents.

Cultural Dance Exploration

Description: Explore traditional dances from different cultures, allowing children to learn and perform them.

Benefits: Encourages cultural appreciation, physical coordination, and an understanding of dance.

Variations: Explore dances from specific cultures.

Landform Models

Description: Create 3D models of geographic landforms like mountains, valleys, and rivers using craft materials.

Benefits: Promotes geographic awareness, spatial understanding, and creativity.

Variations: Explore different landforms.

Social and Emotional Development Activities

Feelings Charades

Description: Children act out different emotions (e.g., happy, sad, angry) without using words. Others guess the emotion being portrayed.

Benefits: Enhances emotional recognition and expression, fosters empathy, and improves communication skills.

Variations: Use picture cards with various emotional expressions, or act out scenarios that trigger different emotions.

Emotion Stones

Description: Paint various emotions (happy, sad, surprised, etc.) on stones. Children can pick a stone and share a time when they felt that emotion.

Benefits: Promotes emotional self-awareness, encourages open communication, and helps children understand that it's okay to feel different emotions.

Variations: Add more nuanced emotions or combine emotions on a single stone (e.g., happy and surprised).

Emotion Cards and Stories

Description: Create emotion cards with facial expressions. Read stories or scenarios, and ask children to match the emotion card to how the character might be feeling.

Benefits: Enhances emotional vocabulary, empathy, and understanding of others' feelings.

Variations: Use real-life photos or illustrations on the cards to depict different emotions.

Gratitude Journal

Description: Provide children with a journal to write or draw something they are thankful for each day.

Benefits: Promotes a positive outlook, self-reflection, and gratitude, which can lead to emotional well-being.

Variations: Encourage children to create a "happiness jar" where they write down daily moments of joy to read later.

Feelings Check-In Circle

Description: Gather in a circle and ask children to share how they're feeling today. Discuss reasons for those emotions in a safe and supportive environment.

Benefits: Encourages emotional expression, active listening, and empathetic responses.

Variations: Use a "feeling wheel" with various emotional words to help children describe their emotions more precisely.

Emotion Masks

Description: Provide blank masks or templates for children to decorate as they feel at the moment. Discuss why they chose specific expressions.

Benefits: Encourages creativity, emotional expression, and self-awareness.

Variations: Use different materials like paper plates or craft foam for the masks, or provide props that represent emotions.

Gratitude Circle

Description: Sit in a circle and have each child express something they are thankful for. Encourage them to think about everyday things that bring joy.

Benefits: Promotes gratitude, mindfulness, and positive thinking.

Variations: Create a gratitude tree by drawing or placing leaves on a tree with what each child is thankful for.

MARIA MONTESSORI'S ORIGINAL LEARNING MATERIAL DESIGNS

Here is a list of relevant learning toys and materials designed by Maria Montessori. If you feel interested in a particular object, I suggest you look it up on the internet to gain more information and images. I encourage you to make DIY versions of these when possible, as they can make a fun activity and allow you to put in your unique personal touch!

Infant and Toddler Materials

   1. Munari Mobile – High-contrast mobile for newborn visual tracking.

   2. Gobbi Mobile – Graduated color mobile to develop color perception.

   3. Octahedron Mobile – Primary-colored mobile for visual development.

   4. Bell on a Ribbon – Hanging bell for cause-effect understanding.

5. Wooden Ring on a Ribbon – Tool to encourage grasping.

6. Interlocking Discs – Wooden discs for hand-to-hand transfer.

7. Object Permanence Box with Tray – Box where a ball disappears and reappears, enhancing object permanence.

8. Object Permanence Box with Drawer – Drawer-based version for additional complexity.

9. Imbucare Box – Box for object insertion to develop hand-eye coordination.

10. Coin Box with Drawer – Coin slot box to improve fine motor skills.

11. Peg Box – Removable pegs to build motor control.

12. Ring Stacker – Stacking rings to encourage problem-solving.

13. Horizontal Dowel – Tool for sliding objects, enhancing coordination.

Practical Life Materials

1. Pouring, Spooning, and Transferring Sets – Tools for fine motor skills.

2. Dressing Frames – Frames with zippers, buttons, laces, etc., for practicing dressing.

3. Cutting Board and Spreader Set – Child-sized tools for food preparation.

Sensorial Materials

1. **Pink Tower** – Set of cubes to develop size discrimination.

2. **Brown Stair** – Rectangular prisms for dimension understanding.

3. **Knobbed Cylinders** – Cylinders to build size and depth perception.

4. **Color Tablets** – Color-matching tablets.

5. **Sound Cylinders** – Cylinders with different sounds to refine auditory skills.

6. **Smelling Jars** – Containers with scents for olfactory exploration.

7. **Thermic Bottles** – Bottles with various temperatures for thermal sense training.

8. **Rough and Smooth Boards** – Boards for tactile refinement.

9. **Geometric Solids** – 3D shapes for spatial awareness.

10. **Baric Tablets** – Weighted tablets for distinguishing weight.

11. **Tasting Bottles** – Bottles with different flavors to develop taste.

12. **Tactile Boards with Varying Textures** – Advanced textured boards for tactile exploration.

13. **Mystery Bag** – Bag with objects for touch identification.

14. **Constructive Triangles** – Triangles used to explore geometric concepts.

Mathematics Materials

1. **Number Rods** – Rods to teach quantity and sequence.

2. **Sandpaper Numbers** – Tactile numbers for learning numeric symbols.

3. **Spindle Box** – Box with numbered compartments for counting.

4. **Numerical Beads and Chains** – Beads for counting and multiplication.

5. **Golden Beads** – Beads representing place value.

6. **Addition, Subtraction, Multiplication, and Division Boards** – Hands-on boards for arithmetic.

7. **Binomial and Trinomial Cubes** – Cubes for understanding algebraic concepts.

8. **Fraction Circles** – Circles to explore fractions.

9. **Dot Game** – Board for practicing addition and multiplication.

10. **Stamp Game** – Tiles representing units, tens, hundreds, and thousands for arithmetic.

11. **Hundred Board and Thousand Chain** – Tools for counting and number sequence learning.

12. Checkerboard for Multiplication – Grid for large-number multiplication.

13. Small Bead Frame and Large Bead Frame – Abacus-like frames for arithmetic operations.

Language Materials

1. Sandpaper Letters – Tactile letters for learning letter formation.

2. Moveable Alphabet – Set of letters for word construction.

3. Metal Insets – Shapes and frames for pencil control.

4. Object and Picture Matching Cards – Cards for vocabulary building.

5. Phonetic Reading Cards – Cards for reading and sound recognition.

6. Grammar Symbols – Color-coded symbols representing parts of speech.

7. Reading Analysis Strips – Strips to analyze and understand sentences.

Cultural and Science Materials

1. Botany and Zoology Puzzles – Puzzles for plants, animals, and anatomy.

2. Geography Puzzle Maps – Maps that introduce continents, countries, and landforms.

3. Land and Water Forms – Models of land and water formations, like islands and lakes.

Music Materials

1. Bells – Bells representing musical scales for pitch and tone exploration.

2. Tone Bars – Metal bars for understanding musical scales.

3. Music Notation Materials – Tools for introducing musical notation and rhythm.

4. Rhythm Instruments – Percussion instruments for rhythm practice.

REFERENCES

Respect for Children as Unique Individuals https://silverlinemontessori.com/the-montessori-method-respect-for-children-as-unique-individuals/

Observation https://montessoriguide.org/observation

Montessori's Gentle Approach To Discipline https://www.montessori.org/montessoris-gentle-approach-to-discipline/

Montessori Freedom within Limits - Toledo https://www.montessoritoledo.org/news-detail?pk=1462103#:~:text=The%20concept%20of%20%22freedom%20within,with%20appropriate%20limits%20and%20structure.

The Absorbent Mind https://montessori150.org/maria-montessori/montessori-books/absorbent-mind

The Absorbent Mind, Maria Montssori, Digital Fire, August 15th, 2023

Sensitive Periods in Montessori Education https://www.trilliummontessori.org/sensitive-periods/

45+ Montessori Sensorial Activities and Materials https://themontessorisite.com/montessori-sensorial/

The Benefits of Nature-Based Learning in Early Childhood https://www.happybunnies.com/the-benefits-of-nature-based-learning-in-early-childhood/

The Montessori Method: Self-Education with Guidance https://parenting.kars4kids.org/montessori-method-self-education-guidance/

DIY Montessori Sensorial & Practical life Materials https://www.makingmontessoriours.com/2011/02/sensorial-practical-life-materials-we.html

a Montessori approach to building intrinsic motivation https://themontessorinotebook.com/a-montessori-approach-to-building-intrinsic-motivation

The Montessori method of education: A child-led approach https://www.daynurseries.co.uk/advice/the-montessori-method-of-education-a-child-led-approach

THE MONTESSORI METHOD: With illustrations, Maria Montessori, Kindle Edition, Nov 21 2018

Dr. Montessori's Own Handbook, Maria Montessori, Kindle Edition, August 20 2016

How Does Montessori Education Develop Cognitive Skills ... https://theglobalmontessorinetwork.org/how-does-montessori-education-foster-the-development-of-cognitive-skills-in-children/

13 Gross Motor Activities Ideas With a Montessori Twist https://montessorigeneration.com/blogs/montessori/gross-motor-activities-ideas?srsltid=AfmBOopvchgbgVrgSV3BkOuTdY-2ZPQG9P2o0uZenByDd59WHSVo7oNS

Practical Life Materials And Tools for the Montessori ... https://printables.montessorinature.com/practical-life-materials-for-montessori/

The Role of Montessori Education in Developing Emotional ... https://www.montessoridowntown.com/the-role-of-montessori-education-in-developing-emotional-intelligence-in-children/

What is the Prepared Environment? Quotes from ... https://www.thekavanaughreport.com/2018/05/what-is-prepared-environment-quotes.html

How (and Why) to Set Up a Montessori Kitchen at Home https://www.greenchildmagazine.com/montessori-kitchen-at-home/

8 Tips to Create a Montessori Bedroom https://woodandhearts.com/blogs/news/montessori-bedroom-ideas?srsltid=AfmBOoptY71Tsff8V-JnbmiEzbs5_njpZKhGuUcIboHEQslxO89faKCR6

Setting Up a Montessori Playroom in your Home https://greenspringmontessori.org/setting-up-a-montessori-playroom-in-your-home/

Maria Montessori Quotes https://amshq.org/About-Montessori/History-of-Montessori/Who-Was-Maria-Montessori/Maria-Montessori-Quotes

The ultimate list of Montessori activities for babies, toddlers ... https://themontessorinotebook.com/montessori-activities-for-babies-toddlers-and-preschoolers

Preparing the Environment at Home https://www.livingmontessori.com/preparing-the-environment-at-home/

How Montessori Parenting Style Can Help You Raise ... https://www.paperpinecone.com/blog/montessori-parenting-style-your-comprehensive-guide-raise-amazing-child

www.ingramcontent.com/pod-product-compliance
Lightning Source LLC
Chambersburg PA
CBHW072000070526
44583CB00015B/1266